A D I V I N E   D U E T

Smyth & Helwys Publishing, Inc.
6316 Peake Road
Macon, Georgia 31210-3960
1-800-747-3016
©2013 by Alicia Davis Porterfield
All rights reserved.
Printed in the United States of America.

The paper used in this publication meets the minimum requirements of
American National Standard for Information Sciences—
Permanence of Paper for Printed Library Materials.
ANSI Z39.48–1984. (alk. paper)

Library of Congress Cataloging-in-Publication Data

A divine duet : ministry and motherhood / edited by Alicia Davis Porterfield.
pages cm
ISBN 978-1-57312-676-2 (pbk. : alk. paper)
1. Women clergy. 2. Women clergy--Family relationships.
3. Families of clergy. 4. Working mothers. I. Porterfield, Alicia Davis.
BV676.D58 2013
253'.22--dc23

2013015804

A Divine Duet

MINISTRY *and* MOTHERHOOD

ALICIA DAVIS PORTERFIELD

editor

Also by
Alicia Davis Porterfield

Proverbs: Living Wisely, Loving Well
(with Eric S. Porterfield)

To the "great cloud of witnesses" who cheers us on,

to the families who make our hearts sing,

and to our God who creates the divine duet of

ministry and motherhood

Acknowledgments

Thank you to all the contributors, who took time out of their full lives as ministers and mothers to participate in this project. Your voices are a gift and a blessing. Thanks for the courage to share your questions and wisdom, struggles and triumphs. Putting our truths on the page is no easy task. Thanks also to the people of Smyth & Helwys for partnering with us on this endeavor.

I thank my husband, Eric, and our three boys: learning and growing with you is a gift beyond measure. I am so grateful for the larger family, mentors, and friends, whom God uses in my life. And thanks be to the God in whom "all shall be well" (Julian of Norwich). Amen.

Contents

Introduction 1

Chapter 1
A Tale of Two Callings 3
Natalie Nicholas Adams

Chapter 2
Princess Tara..9
Katrina Stipe Brooks

Chapter 3
A Place Near Your Altar 15
Stacey Sandifer Buford

Chapter 4
✳ Letting Go 21
Jenny Frazier Call

Chapter 5
They, She, and Thou Art with Me 29
Stephanie Little Coyne

Chapter 6
Ministry, Motherhood, and Messes 35
Griselda Escobar

Chapter 7
A Time for Every Purpose..41
Nicole Finkelstein-Blair

Chapter 8
Other People's Children: Salome and Motherhood....47
Jenny Folmar

Chapter 9
Once Upon a Time: The Tale of a
Not-So-Wicked Stepmother 53
Kerrie Clayton Jordan

Chapter 10
Nurturing Life: A Mother-Theologian Reflects..........................61
    Nora O. Lozano

Chapter 11
Reverend Doctor Mom 67
    Courtney Lyons

Chapter 12
The Crazy Beautiful: Raising Our Family in the Inner City 75
    Angel Pittman

Chapter 13
A Limp, a Blessing, and a New Name....................................83
    Alicia Davis Porterfield

Chapter 14
A Journey to Family 89
    Susie C. Reeder

Chapter 15
Summer and Sacraments 95
    Holly Sprink

Chapter 16
Mom or Minister? 101
    Amy R. Stertz

Chapter 17
Pregnant and Remembered Hopes 107
    Meredith J. Stone

Chapter 18
The Photograph 113
    Melanie Kilby Storie

Chapter 19
Grace and Hope..119
    Virginia Ross Taylor

Chapter 20
"That's Life!" 123
    Kristin Adkins Whitesides

INTRODUCTION

Alicia Davis Porterfield

Our Scriptures resound with stories of call and stories of birth. Both are essential to the people of God. The account of Abram's call in Genesis 12 involves a birth story, too. In order for him to become a "great nation," someone has to give birth to the babies who will populate that nation.

Later in the narrative, when infertility plagues Abraham and Sarah, we hear some of Sarah's struggle around becoming a mother (Gen 16:1-16). Finally, God sends hope, promising that she will give birth to a son, though she is far "advanced in age" (18:11). When Isaac is born, Sarah marvels, "Who would ever have said to Abraham that Sarah would nurse children?" (21:7).

The child she bore allowed Abraham to become "Father Abraham." Becoming a mother changed Sarah from someone who laughed in derision at God's promise to someone who laughed with delight at God's goodness (18:12-15; 21:6). Her call to follow God with Abraham and her call to become Isaac's mother shaped her life and our collective faith story.

This "duet" of calls, to follow God and to become a mother, continues in God's people today. In moderate Baptist life, as more women follow God's call into ministry, many are discovering the power of this duet. These women are gifted for ministry, trained and shaped through excellent educations, and affirmed in their call, most often through ordination. They serve as pastors in churches, on campuses, in impoverished areas, prisons, hospitals, hospices, the military, and in academia. And many of them are also called to be mothers: birth mothers, adoptive mothers, mothers to other people's children, mothers to their students. As they continue to follow God, the call story and the birth story combine, and the duet rings true.

Honoring this duet of calls may be some of the most important work minister-mothers do. It certainly has been so in my life as a minister and a mother of three young boys. Following God's call into ministry turned my life upside down; following God's call into motherhood turned it inside out.

But I found few spaces in which to reflect on and honor this holy duet. At conferences, workshops, and denominational gatherings, I found myself having numerous conversations with other mother-ministers. Leaning against the wall in the hallways, we pondered the changes in our lives, the shifts in identity and priorities created by becoming mothers-who-are-ministers. We gathered in little knots, old friends from divinity school or internships sharing everything from nursing advice and preaching ideas to adoption pointers. In impromptu meetings, we celebrated the gift of new life even as we struggled with the different roles this new calling required. Though each of our stories was unique, the common threads of ministry and motherhood linked us together.

In my own wilderness, this strange land of motherhood and ministry, God used these connections to make a new way for me. While I wrote regularly about this new identity in a journal and prayed almost without ceasing for guidance, what really helped me was the sharing of others' stories. Out of that longing to honor these stories of ministry and motherhood, the dream of this collection was born. Given a mother-minister's schedule, it took a while for the dream to come to fruition. But help and support came from many sources, the invitations to write went out, and these twenty essays came together.

Every essay is as different as the mother-minister who penned it, from theologians to chaplains, inner-city ministers to rural-poverty ministers, youth pastors to preachers, mothers who have adopted, birthed, and done both. The chance to read the essays and interact with their authors has been a holy time for me. Knowing that there are hundreds of equally moving ministry-motherhood stories out there is inspiring.

I pray that we will begin intentionally incorporating these sacred stories of ministry and motherhood into our larger church life. I pray that this collection shapes our conversations, our prayers, our churches, and our awareness of minister-mothers. May God's people honor both: the call story and the birth story, ministry and motherhood—a divine duet.

CHAPTER 1

A TALE OF TWO CALLINGS

Natalie Nicholas Adams

On May 25, 1986, I was ordained into the gospel ministry at The First Baptist Church of Forsyth, Georgia. With one more year of seminary remaining, I was single and twenty-five years old. Hoping to get a position in campus ministry, I knew that door was closing fast with denominational changes. The ordination council was composed of twelve men and no women. The two-hour inquisition focused mainly on theology and ministerial gifts. After an additional hour's wait in the hall, I was invited to sit before the counsel and hear what I assumed was a *no*. The senior pastor said they were conflicted about whether to ordain me—not because they questioned my calling but because they knew how hard it would be to be an ordained female minister in Southern Baptist life. I almost passed out when they said the vote was a unanimous *yes!*

Thinking that ordination would be my biggest hurdle, I was confident and excited about following God's call wherever it would lead. With rose-colored glasses and a big bucket of hope (and faith), I was ready to face both the challenges and joys that lay ahead of me. I expected to encounter certain "brick walls": having the "wrong plumbing" (as a female), churches not being ready for a woman minister, or the perception that it was inappropriate for a single woman to work with the male pastor. But at age thirty-five, it was the birth of my first child that caused me to resign my position as Associate Pastor of Central Baptist Church in Newnan, Georgia. No one was more shocked at my decision than I was!

When I turned thirty and was still single, I accepted the fact that marriage was not in the cards for me. Being single allowed me the freedom to give 100 percent of my time and energy to enjoying ministry, which I did immensely. Church positions included working with every age group through Christian education, pastoral care, and preaching. In every ministry position I filled, I was the first female. I never had the opportunity to work with fellow female clergy. It wasn't until I was married and expecting my first child that I even thought to ask if there was a maternity clause in the personnel policies. There wasn't. My only lifeline was the Baptist Women in Ministry groups in North Carolina and Georgia. Thank God for that wonderful group of women! But when it came to dating, getting married, and having a family, I had no mentors. I didn't think I needed one because I thought as I always had: *my life would have to come second to my ministry.*

Part of my personal ministry ethics guidelines included the rule that I would not date a church member. I believed that situation created a conflict of interest, and if the relationship went sour for either party the church would be hurt. Thus I never saw church members as potential dating partners. So when I had a dream one night that the leader of the Singles' group at church kissed me, I awoke with the joy and surprise that I was in love.

Tony and I dated secretly for several months, and eighteen months later we were married. Dating publicly was difficult at times. We would travel out of town to go to dinner, and every time we entered a restaurant I scanned the room looking for church members! Please understand that this was *my* rule, not Tony's and not the church's. Some people in the church wholeheartedly supported our relationship and our privacy, while others did not approve or saw it as a threat to my ministry.

Tony's strength helped me get past all this. He never cared what people said or thought; it was none of their business. It was the first time I felt that someone "had my back" in ministry. Tony has a deep faith and considered entering the ministry many times before he met me. He was an executive with an "outside" job and therefore off limits to "inside" church ridicule and behavioral codes. It made no difference to me that he was a contractor, but it took Tony a long time to decide if he was willing to become a "pastor's wife" (his terminology). He understood what was expected of him and recognized the scrutiny that was about to be placed on his involvement in the church and outside the church.

It was great that Tony loved the church as much as I did. The first two years of marriage and church work went well. He worked long hours. I worked long hours. Then we received word from my doctor that if we were going to have children, the window was open. He didn't know how long the possibility would exist, however, because of major back surgery I had soon after Tony and I married.

The plan was that I would continue serving as associate pastor and, in my forties, possibly accept a call to pastor. My husband and I looked into hiring an au pair (a student nanny from another country), as several working moms were doing in the church. I imagined setting up a playpen in my office for times when I would work late or my husband was out of town. I wasn't keen on using a childcare center. During that time, it didn't dawn on me to ask what options the church might be willing to make to accommodate my soon-to-be-born daughter. But the decision was made for me when, in passing one day, my mother-in-law informed me that she was looking forward to quitting her job and raising her first grandchild. Her words hit me in the gut. I thought, *If I don't want my own mother-in-law to raise my child, then why would I let a total stranger care for her?*

I took a long and realistic look at my life. The previous year, I calculated that I was gone from home twenty-eight days and worked on average four nights a week. The icing on the cake was that my husband's job had no flexibility whatsoever, requiring twelve hours of him most days.

I realized I couldn't have it all. I didn't want my daughter to be passed around from sitter to sitter; after all, I loved this child and I wanted to raise her myself. I felt that I had no options. Without discussing the dilemma with my husband, I announced that I planned to resign from the church and stay home with our daughter and raise her myself. My husband was shocked, the church was shocked, and, in retrospect, I let a lot of people down with my last-minute, no-warning resignation. And on top of that, I made the decision to leave the church so the new minister would have an easier transition. I made these decisions without consulting other moms in ministry or my senior pastor, let alone my own husband! I believed that I had no choice.

It has been my experience that when God has given me plenty of opportunities to make a change and I don't listen or heed, then God makes the change for me. And this is usually a painful lesson. I never wanted the church to be a place that would make my children jealous. So many preachers' kids grow up hating what their mother or father did for a living. Preachers' kids live in a glass bowl—every behavior is held up for praise or discipline. In a way, it is similar to being a celebrity. Church members act like paparazzi, quickly passing along their approval or disapproval of how the children are being raised and the way they act. Not every preacher's kid has a negative experience growing up in the church; every once in a while some of them turn out fine. But just as many churches place the same unreal expectations on the minister's spouse, the family as a whole often needs to be protected and defended.

I was thirty-five years old when our first child was born, so motherhood was hard enough, but balancing motherhood and full-time ministry was too much for me. Knowing what I know now, I believe I made a wise decision. In this one area, I was not ready or willing to be a *pastoral pioneer* as the first female clergy to raise a family while working full-time. I do find it interesting that when I resigned, the church hired another female associate pastor. Within two years, she and her husband had their first child. She resigned before the child was born. The next hired minister was a male.

Our daughter was born two days before the 1996 Olympics in Atlanta, and our son followed sixteen months later. I volunteered at a local church as a layperson in Sunday school, choir, and Vacation Bible School. I missed working in the church every day! It was not an easy transition to leave the clergy world I knew and loved. It wasn't postpartum depression; it was the question of what to do with my brain. I started writing almost immediately. I was fortunate to have several writing contracts with Christian publishers. I stayed active in the Women in Ministry group in Georgia. I brought my children to the meetings. It didn't dawn on me until years later that I was the only one who did that.

Two years later, our family moved, and we became active in a church that I had previously served and that had just called a new pastor—a friend of mine from seminary. It was the first time that we chose a church home as a family. I soon became the volunteer minister of education, and my husband became chair of the deacons. It was a perfect fit for our young family. As a volunteer, if one of my children were sick, I didn't have to take off work as a vacation Sunday. I enjoyed the freedom of ministry without the restraints of dealing with the personnel committee. And my husband didn't have to be in my shadow and was enjoying his ministry. The only glitch was that the church was a forty-five-minute drive from our home. (Moderate Baptist churches are sometimes hard to find.)

Our hardest and yet most joy-filled time as a minister and family was when we became church planters in our own community. The timing seemed perfect. Our youngest was in kindergarten, and the Adams family was in full-time ministry together. The thrill of being part of a church plant is beyond description. As a pastor, I loved being the presence of Christ and having the opportunity to utilize all my gifts and calling. As a wife, it was incredible to work with my husband and see him be part of something bigger than himself. As a mother, I marveled that my children thought it was cool having *their own church* and loved seeing it grow. How often does a mother get to baptize her own children?

When it was good, it was very good . . . but when it was bad, it was very bad. We no longer had family events. Everything was scheduled around the church and its needs. The lines of separation no longer existed. As the church began to unravel, so did our family. Whether we knew it at the time or not, my husband and I needed to choose between keeping the church open or keeping our family together. While we felt like King Solomon deciding how to divide a baby between two mothers, we chose our family. The loss felt as great as losing a child—for all of us.

Three months after the church was closed, our daughter was diagnosed with an inoperable brain tumor. Our daughter Alison has always had health concerns. When she was two and a half, she had a CT scan for her sinuses, and the radiologist came to the recovery room immediately to tell us that we needed to see a neurosurgeon. Alison needed surgery to remove a tumor that had grown around the artery in her brain. After that procedure, her health continued to be complex and bizarre. A "well-meaning" church member once asked me to breakfast only to suggest that our daughter's health problems were self-induced! Our hearts were torn apart again when our daughter's latest brain MRI showed a new inoperable brain tumor in her thalamus. As I write, our now sixteen-year-old beauty is being tested for seizures.

Once again, I am a mother first. These days, I enjoy writing and also serving as an occasional supply preacher. My health has not always been great, and three years ago I was diagnosed with a bone marrow disease that involves weekly infusions and a weakened immune system. My current status would be described as medically retired. Every celebration and milestone is cherished.

Our fifteen-year-old son, Samuel, is so full of life and joy. He sings lead and plays the guitar, hits a mean golf ball, and has a contagious heart for God! Both children are growing in their faith in a wonderful United Methodist church. They often ask why I don't preach anymore. It is a season of rest and worship for me. When I'm filling out those pesky forms in a doctor's office and am asked for my occupation, it is with some sadness that I respond *homemaker*, for my life is so much richer and fuller than that one word implies.

My parents always encouraged me to follow my dreams and not to let obstacles get in my way. Education and career were the criteria by which success was measured. I am thankful for the support I was given, but I can't help wondering how different my life would have been if family were my goal from the beginning. Did it need to get to the point where I had to choose between motherhood or ministry? Is balance possible? Or should family always come first?

It's not easy when you're on vacation and get a call that the chair of deacons passed away. While I was pregnant with our first child, I worked full-time and finished my doctoral dissertation, and it was Advent! I started to have complications and was ordered on bed rest for about two weeks until the bleeding stopped. The church understood and genuinely was concerned, but I still got calls and worked from home as well. Even though I am now medically retired from active ministry, I still find myself having to choose between family and ministry.

The last chapter of motherhood and ministry is yet to come for me. I miss working in the church every day. Being a mother and a wife is a great blessing and joy. My two greatest passions have provided an abundant life for which I am so thankful and completely humbled. I just wish I could have lived them simultaneously.

Rev. Dr. Natalie Nicholas Adams lives in Cumming, Georgia, with husband Tony, two teenage children, and a Yorkie. After receiving a BS in Chemistry and Biology, she earned a MDiv from The Southern Baptist Seminary and a DMin from Columbia Presbyterian Theological Seminary. In addition to Clinical Pastoral Education, international coursework, and writing for various publications, Natalie served churches in North Carolina and Georgia. Now blessed with two teenagers, she asks forgiveness from any parent of a youth that she had the audacity to criticize! Her life's purpose: "Live well. Live blessed."

Chapter 2

Princess Tara

Katrina Stipe Brooks, the Princess's Mommy

Tara was born into our family at a critical time. She entered the world destined to distract us from a very real truth: Tony's father, Pawpaw, was dying. Born while Pawpaw was on a heart transplant list, Tara learned to walk in ICU waiting rooms. Tara was gifted in her role as distractor and lived her life as the center of our attention. Always the princess, this beautiful girl had a way of smiling that pierced the darkness. Tara drew people to her and, in her own way, served as a beacon of hope. Yet despite her magic and her charm, her beloved Pawpaw died when she was sixteen months old, and her Pop, my father, had died two months earlier. A whole new grief set in as our family began to cope with the deaths of both the Brooks and Stipe patriarchs—a grief Tara was destined to lessen in true princess form.

As she grew up, Tara delighted in everyone she met. Born to be an ambassador, she shattered barriers with her intelligence, her gift of hospitality, her huge heart . . . and her courage. Due to the tightening of her Achilles tendons, Tara had walked on her toes since infancy and soon became the favorite target for the unkindness at which children excel. In seventh grade, after a battery of tests, she taught herself how to walk again following bi-lateral tendon lengthening surgery. A twenty-three-hour outpatient experience, her surgery netted her two casts that she wore for six weeks. After surgery on Friday, she was back in school on Monday with the assistance of a wheelchair. Her courage sparked renewed appreciation by her peers, and she flourished.

In high school, Tara announced she wanted to be an ambassador. Encouraging her was not a challenge as she had proven over and over again that she had those gifts. Our mantra became, "We can see you do that! You just need to pray about which venue your ambassadorship will take." Tara thrived in high school. As a gifted, articulate, and confident young woman, she often found herself criticized by less secure peers. Annually, Tara was awarded for her accomplishments in athletics, community service, after-school activities, and classroom performance. Again, her success sometimes made her a mark for the petty jealousies rampant in high school. Many a day she returned home in tears.

The hardest days were ones where the tears were a result of an adult comment. How does one explain hurtful words, uttered by insecure adults, to someone who knows adults are supposed to be above such things? How do you comfort your "princess" when your colleagues hurl comments worse than the ones from her peers? At the same time, Tara's ankles and tendons began to give her problems, and she spent many a day wearing a brace.

Tara entered Oxford College of Emory University in fall 2008. After an incredible summer with Passport Camps on the kids' team, Tara dove into her college experience. Her circle of friends broadened. While she had always seemed at home with people of all types and backgrounds, it was a joy to watch her experience diversity firsthand. She was becoming a people's princess.

Tara had plans. After graduation from Emory University, she was headed to graduate school for a degree in International Relations followed by a PhD. She toyed with the idea of going to Duke for her master's and adding a Master of Divinity. When asked why, she couldn't completely explain it. It was a degree she simply needed to have.

As graduation grew closer, Tara's tendons became more of a physical challenge. In fall 2010, Tara once again had surgery, and this time, at twenty years old, she taught herself how to walk amid her classes. She spent six weeks on pain medicine as she learned, but she maintained a B-average semester. During her recovery, Tara wrestled with her calling. She "settled" some questions and carved out a different ambassador-related path: she was headed into student affairs. This time she would pursue a master's in student affairs followed by a PhD, but she also insisted that an MDiv was necessary for working with collegians.

Two summers ago, following her fourth summer on a PASSPORT *kids* team, I picked her up after a retreat. With tears in her eyes, she shared what God was doing in her life. Listening to her epiphany, my tears flowed freely, but I wasn't prepared for her announcement. I knew seminary was a part of her future plans, but God in God's way had called her name and given her the next step in her journey: she was headed to seminary in the fall.

All along, I knew Tara would go to seminary. Call it a mommy's intuition. Call it being sensitive and aware. Call it what you want, but as I watched our daughter become an adult, I saw God prepare a woman for ministry. In response to her question, "Who would've thought I would go to seminary?" I replied quietly, "I did." The reality of her revelation started to sink in as she called her dad and shared her epiphany. In spite of the miles, I could "see" his face. He was just as shocked at her decision and plan as I was.

Then the questions began to swirl in my heart.

How do you tell your beloved princess that this call she is following will not be easy? How do you begin to share the pain of following your call in a world that insists a woman has certain boundaries? How do you prepare your daughter for all the men who will receive invitations to join church staffs just because they are men, in spite of her being perhaps the most qualified in the room? And more important, how do you say those things out loud to your princess, one who was spiritually formed on your watch and taught that God calls, God equips, and God provides.

Maybe if I hadn't been to seminary myself, it wouldn't be as much of a challenge. Maybe if I didn't know firsthand how Tara will be challenged and fashioned and formed by some of the world's most creative critical thinkers and ministers, if I didn't know how she will be edified and encouraged, empowered and equipped at seminary—maybe then I could pretend that her road will be different from my own.

But the truth I discovered is this: ministry is a challenge for women. Not all churches and ministries are open to women. For a woman, following God into ministry takes following your call amid some of the most awful, non-Christian words and actions by folks who extrapolate Scripture to create their orthodox doctrine. It takes smiling and being Christ when you are cast as the reason the world is going to hell in a handbasket. It takes recreating yourself to survive financially without resentment as inadequate men are chosen over you. It takes trusting God so completely that, more often than not, you have no "clue" as to how or what God is doing to carve a way for you in ministry. It takes the courage to say yes to ministry opportunities you may have never considered before or are outside your comfort zone. It takes being able to survive a reputation ruined by insecure individuals and ministering alongside those who defame you while still trusting that, even in the chaos, God is doing something so spectacular that the current reality is not only a preparation but also part of the journey—even amid the tears and pain.

How can I prepare my daughter, our princess, for ministry without discouraging her? How do I, as a seasoned disciple, continue to encourage and edify our daughter for a difficult journey? How do I prepare our daughter for the moment in time when her male peers graduate to become part of the system and no longer "remember" her? How do I applaud our princess without shattering her world?

Welcome to my new reality. I find myself wrestling with what role I should play now that my greatest fear has come to fruition. As one who has wanted to protect her princess from the dragons in the world, how do I as a wounded pilgrim fashion a role in my daughter's spiritual formation? As our princess's mommy, how do I remain present for her and yet know that all the kisses and hugs will not heal the pain that comes with this journey? How do I remain faithful to my own call and welcome her into an adventure that has so much joy, so much pain, and so many tears that I wouldn't trade it for the world?

Perhaps that is my starting point. In spite of the pain, unemployment, silence by my once encouraging male peers, intentional dismissal, and gossip and ignorant "rantings" about the role of women in the church, I would not change my call. The God who called me also sustains me and guides me as I process disappointments, pain, and betrayal. I am stronger than I was and more determined to follow my call, whatever that means. I am more centered and even more compassionate. I am more discerning and am able to distinguish between ignorance and malice. And while I have absolutely no clue what God is doing in my life right now, I know God is fashioning something spectacular: something I cannot see, but it has a fragrance so sweet that I cannot fathom its glory.

Maybe this is where being a mommy stops and being a disciple begins. Maybe I just need to trust the process. Maybe I just need to cheer Tara on as others cheered me on. Maybe I just need to enjoy her journey, knowing that I have firsthand knowledge of pain should she ever need a shoulder to cry on, but also firsthand knowledge of the joy of it all.

Perhaps Tara's entire journey, from struggles to triumphs, has prepared her for this moment. And while it is easy to pledge support when it is someone else's child, this is a new season for me—a new journey. A journey that God will use to fashion and form, equip and edify, empower and encourage us to be the women God needs us to be in this world: beacons of hope, conduits of love, and icons of grace.

Lord, let it be so.

In addition to being Princess Tara's mommy, **Rev. Katrina Stipe Brooks** *is the proud mom of Joseph, an accounting/finance major and an offensive lineman at Maryville College. Katrina's husband, Tony, is employed with the Virginia Baptist Mission Board as a field strategist and Sunday school specialist. A graduate of Samford University and Baptist Theological Seminary at Richmond, Katrina serves as campus pastor for Lynchburg Christian Fellowship at Lynchburg College and as interim youth pastor at Madison Heights Baptist Church.*

CHAPTER 3

A PLACE NEAR YOUR ALTAR

Stacey Sandifer Buford

"Even the sparrow has found a home and the swallow a nest for herself, where she may have her young—a place near your altar" (Psalm 84:3).

The hospital bed stretched beneath me, cradling me and the tiny daughter who had come into my life in a whirlwind some months before. I settled back against the warm blankets the nurses brought and opened my arms to hold my frightened child. I would not think about the pictures they would take . . . pictures of my child's heart. For today, I would not let my own fears set in.

They settled her toddler frame against me, her back against my abdomen. Tiny shoulders and precious head tucked neatly under my rib cage. She settled into my lap as if we were one body, one soul. The length of her body, tiny for her age, barely spanned the length of my pelvis. My hips cradled and supported her as the lights were dimmed and the dark screen of the echo machine came into view. As the green patterns of my daughter's life rhythm emerged, our breathing fell together, and I could feel our heartbeats in sync.

My arms went instinctively around my middle so full of this child and this moment. In awe, I watched the patterns of her heartbeat, strong and steady, and was intensely thankful. It was a rare moment of physicality, being one body with this child who had grown under another rib cage and been held throughout her first year of life by another mother. Could I really have thought just a few short months ago that life would be the same when my third child came home to us? That another adoption would not somehow permanently tip the balance of the universe, altering the shape of my world as a mom and a minister?

Truth be told, the shape of my world as a mother had been as difficult to imagine as my face as a Baptist woman in ministry. It was not a lack of clarity or desire on my part. In fact, becoming both a mother and a minister were twin dreams in my heart, utterly intertwined and inseparable, placed so closely together in my being that I can no longer remember the mysterious force that placed them there. Equal parts passion and call led me to calmly explain at the age of seventeen that my life's ambition was to complete a bachelor's degree, attend seminary, prepare to be a missionary, and have a family. My senior high self smiled and said, "I look forward to combining family life and ministry." The words rolled off my tongue as if I were announcing a double major for my life whose compatibility was an unexamined and assumed given. That both motherhood and ministry would happen was as indisputable as my very life and existence, because both were absolute expressions of who I understood myself to be in the world. What I would look like as a mother and as a minister was harder to flesh out.

Newly married and enrolled in seminary with my husband, I had imagined an immensely pregnant me proudly walking across the stage of my denomination's flagship seminary, proclaiming with my presence the absolute truth that God did, in fact, call women to minister in all of our reproducing glory. Further, I would pause, accept my hard-won Master of Divinity degree, and then walk gracefully across the stage, head out the door, and proceed directly to the local labor and delivery, where I would birth the child whose entry into the world had been perfectly timed to take place after finals and before the start of my first full-time call.

Despite my early certainty, neither becoming a mother nor becoming a minister came easily. I dove headlong with my inseparable dreams of ministry and motherhood into the sea of denominational turmoil and personal infertility. Progress came to a grinding halt. The simultaneous graduation and birth celebration of my imagination was replaced by longing and yearning. My longing to become the mother of my particular children was matched in intensity only by my longing to become a minister, to be fully welcomed, claimed, and celebrated by the people of faith who had nurtured my life and growth.

I struggled to reconcile my images of myself with the very real path I was walking. Images of me glowing and pregnant in robes and stole were replaced by the reality of sweating over reams of autobiographical statements for three adoption home studies while completing a master's degree, becoming a resident chaplain, seeking denominational endorsement, and moving into my first staff chaplain position.

Five years of infertility had given way in a joyous rush. We had adopted three children in the span of two and a half years and now breathlessly paused to see what life as parents would be like. Almost simultaneously, a decade of longing for a place near God's altar culminated in my first years of service as a clinical chaplain. It was the stuff of dreams. My life was now full of what I was sure would be equal parts diapers, bottles, rocking chairs, and interdisciplinary rounds. Equipped with a calendar and a partner committed to co-everything, I set out to sketch my landscape of motherhood and ministry. If the blank pages of my calendar were the imprint of my life, it seemed to me that finding a new sense of balance would be as simple as blocking in enough boxes dedicated to work and enough boxes dedicated to parenting. What I did not imagine was that the passions of my life would not fit in boxes and that the boundaries around motherhood and ministry would not be as distinct as a penciled line on my calendar.

Holding my tiny daughter and watching her heart beat, I was fully immersed in the uncertainty of life and parenting. The combined need of my three *precious* children settled into my being on that day, and something inside me shifted permanently and irrevocably. There would be no balance, no imaginary divide between myself as a minister and myself as a mother, no careful combining of equal parts family life and ministry. In that moment, I knew that my children were a part of my fiber, the weight of their presence and their need adding substance and color to the threads of my life. I knew that neither their gifts to me nor their need for me could be contained in the boxes of my calendar or the imaginings of my mind. No matter what else I might be or do in the world, I was their mother, and their need would shape the structure of my life and work.

The structure of a life and work is as unique as a fingerprint. It flows from who we are and the choices we make at key moments in time. It becomes a matter of public record, this solid chain of what we give ourselves over to. Yet the path to understanding oneself as a minister is as private as that to becoming a mother. I cannot say with exactness the moment when I knew with undeniable certainty that I was a minister in my very fiber. It did not come in the ways I expected, though each of the traditional milestones of ministry did eventually weave themselves into my life. It did not come when I finally walked across the stage with tears of relief and exhilaration to accept that dreamed of Master of Divinity degree. It did not come when I came out on the other side of a Clinical Pastoral Education residency, grounded and at home in my skin. It did not come when I prayerfully knelt beneath the weight of familiar hands reaching out to claim me and affirm God's call on my life in ordination. And it did not even come in the moments of sharing sacred space with people in tender moments of ministry. It came instead from the depths of my most private moments as a mother.

From the beginning, I had loved the work of coming alongside and being with others. I loved the art of creating spaces for folks and of juxtaposing the complexity of sacred text and the complicated messiness of real life. I loved the way my work carried me: pushing, pulling, and prodding me beyond myself. For over a decade, I cobbled together a structure of life and work, caring for the unique needs of my children and for others, creating spaces for patients to do soul work and spaces for my family to grow and learn and become.

And then life took a cataclysmic shift. The combined needs of our family and the work that I loved began to pull at each other. The spaces for growing and healing became crowded and cluttered, pushed aside by logistics and sheer need. I responded from the depths of my being and let go of my work. I pried free the fingers that clung tightly to my "place" as a minister, that clutched my position in this world, and I quietly came home.

As often happens in periods of medical crisis, survival needs became paramount. Food, clothing, and shelter for our family were the nucleus of my life and work. The immediacy of the physical care needs for our children at this particular juncture rivaled that of their newborn and toddler days. The sheer exhaustion of nurturing and providing and the chronic nature of special needs settled into my bones. I struggled with isolation and grief punctuated by moments of sheer joy at being with my children. I wanted more than anything to soak in the precious moments of parenting the three of them. I had longed to give in to the rhythm of my family's need, to be carried away and totally absorbed in the flow of being with my family. So, even amid the exhaustion, I was intensely thankful to be home.

I did not grieve for the job I left. Instead, I grieved for the sense of knowing I had a place near the altar of God. I missed imagining the flow and the progression of a life and a career. I missed the markers of professional goals set and accomplished. I longed for the illusion that I knew where I was going and where the river of God's guidance might be carrying me. So, like the psalmist in Psalm 84, I alternately basked in the beauty of God's dwelling, inhabiting these moments of parenting, and yearned for a formal place of service (no matter how lowly) in the courts of the Lord.

Many months into this journey of immersion in parenting, I found myself by the hospital bed of my son. It took me back to the moment years ago when I held my daughter in the midst of her physical need and knew that I was a mother. It had been years since I had struggled to understand myself as a parent. Those questions had long since disappeared in the wake of sleepless nights, bedtime stories, and first lost teeth. I sat quietly beside my sleeping son and felt the unknowns that no combination of careful parenting or medical science can push away. I sat with the uncertainty of life, quietly bearing witness to its goodness in that moment. "Better is one day in your courts than a thousand elsewhere" (Ps 84:10). I was intensely grateful for the gift of being this child's mother. I had no idea where his needs would take us as a family or where our combined family need would lead us next.

Perhaps that was the moment when I recognized myself. The call to be with the other in the midst of life's uncertainty, bearing witness to the indwelling of God, washed over me. It was a skin that wrapped itself around my marrow, never leaving me and giving my life shape both as a mother and as a minister. This call did not overtake me in the course of a job or a role. It could not be contained in a position or a title. It was a call that changed who I was as a mother in that moment. I was in my very fiber a minister, a doorkeeper in the house of God, and simultaneously a mother building a nest and raising her young. Whatever twists and turns might come, I would forever be a servant in the courts of the Lord. Like the sparrow, I recognized myself to be at home. Like the swallow, I had found a place near God's altar that could not be defined by a job as a minister or by my work as a mother. It was the skin of my call that would give structure to my life and work. I had found my place, deep inside, and I was at last home.

Rev. Stacey Sandifer Buford is a chaplain by trade and a mother by the miracle of adoption. She earned her BA in Religious Education from Samford University and her MDiv at Columbia Theological Seminary. Call has been a driving force, leading her down hospital halls, into local pulpits, and through doors of nonprofit organizations into the broader community. Her husband is Jon Buford, and together they are the parents of LeighAnne, Savannah, and Will. The Bufords live in middle Tennessee.

CHAPTER 4

LETTING GO

Jenny Frazier Call

As a type-A, honor-student, perfectionism-driven woman, I have always had a great need to feel in control. If I follow a certain path, I assume I will get the results I desire. And yet, in ministry and motherhood, this is not guaranteed. My life on these dual paths is teaching me that "success" in either realm is more about surrender than control.

I dropped yet another to-do list onto the kitchen table as we left for what we believed was a routine pregnancy checkup. There were a dozen more items to cross off, and with two weeks remaining, I felt we were in decent shape. Everything had gone according to plan so far. I had followed health and dietary recommendations meticulously (no sprouts! no lunch meat! no sushi! lots of protein!), and the *What to Expect* book was worn and dog-eared from my nightly reading. Little did I know that I was in for my first big lesson of parenthood: *I am not in control.*

My husband, John, and I went into the doctor's office as excited parents-to-be, although I was a little wearier from the wear of pregnancy and feeling crampy. I was anxious to have an ultrasound and once again see the little life developing within me. In my eager anticipation, I was unprepared for the doctor's concern after consulting with the ultrasound technician, and surprised at his insistence on doing his own check and a non-stress test (what an oxymoron—a test to determine the health of your pregnancy being named "non-stress"). We were clueless about the process but understood that something wasn't right and the measurements weren't adding up. This precious baby, who was perfect in every way in our minds and dreams, was too small, and I, inconceivably, was in the early stages of labor.

The doctor calmly but firmly told us to head straight to the hospital for another check. "Do not pass go, do not collect $200." At the time, we were more concerned with the details of who would feed our dogs that afternoon and the disappointment of forgoing our planned ice cream stop after the doctor visit to consider the possible implications. We had done everything right. What could possibly go wrong? At the hospital, we laughed as we parked in the stork parking for labor and delivery patients, feeling like we were cheating the system. In the labor and delivery unit, my information was quickly taken, my vitals were recorded, and I was situated in a room. It wasn't until they put the ID band around my wrist and the on-call doctor stepped into the room that I realized something was amiss.

They had been waiting for us and were well prepared for what was in store. Somehow we had missed the memo. We had expected to go home after another retest, but the doctor informed us that I would either be having a baby that evening or in the morning, depending on the severity of the situation. Her results also showed a baby around five pounds, which measured size-wise about four weeks earlier than his actual gestation. Even worse, there was little amniotic fluid due to holes in my placenta, which had begun breaking down prematurely. The baby was in distress, and with each cramp (which I now understood to be a contraction), the baby's heart rate was decelerating. An emergency C-section was in order.

The doctor tried to keep everything light, joking as she wheeled me to the operating room and asking if my husband would be all right. There was music playing and casual conversation. And yet we didn't know the severity of what we faced. Would our baby boy be okay? How would this first surgery affect me? What care would our small son require if he survived at all? How could we handle it? We were numb with shock and fear. Although my husband and I were both ministers, I don't remember any prayers other than an internal plea of "Please . . . ." I didn't even know what to ask.

I remember feeling the tugging as the doctor worked to deliver my baby, a battle my numb body was subjected to, a struggle that I bore and yet could not control. I had to submit our fate to others and trust in providence and wisdom beyond my own. As the doctor pulled the life from within me, there was the announcement of the time of Brady's birth and, to our relief, a tiny and brief cry. The nurse brought our son over for us to see, and his eyes met ours, staring intently and calmly, as we drank in his features and murmured our hellos in the brief moments before they rushed him off for more care. John followed Brady and the medical staff to the nursery while my visible brokenness was patched up before I was sent to recovery.

I was alone in the quiet, cold recovery room when a true sense of powerlessness overtook me. I literally could not move, even though I tried to will myself into movement, knowing that my release and reunion with my family was dependent on the feeling returning to my body. But while my body was numb of feeling, my heart was not. I was now a mother, and my thoughts went beyond myself to my new family.

It seemed like days before a nurse brought back some Polaroid pictures that my husband had taken of our boy, and lifetimes before I was reunited with John, who told me what had been happening. His face shone with pride, and my fear was somewhat relieved. Brady was tiny but holding his own. As time went on, there were thoughts of sending him to a NICU at another hospital, but he always bounced back. There were periods when they thought to give him oxygen, and then his breathing would get stronger. For every fear, there was momentary relief before another issue would surface. He was blessed to be as healthy as he was with no life-threatening complications, but we felt like we were treading water, uncertain of what our new "normal" would be.

I was perplexed that none of my planning had prevented this. My eating plan had not ensured a healthy baby, nor had my regular doctor's visits and prenatal care prepared us for the possibility of any problems. My faith, my vocation as a minister (in a dual-minister family!), had not insulated us from adversity. I had followed all the right steps and was now at a loss of what to do. As I watched my baby struggle, I was powerless to help . . . or so I thought. On one of our pediatrician's regular visits to our room to check in, the doctor sensed our frustration at the one-step-forward, two-steps-back nature of Brady's "progress" and gently asked whether we would like to pray together. This was one of many sacred moments in our journey of early parenthood when we stopped to recognize our helplessness and instead trust in God's protection and care of us. You would think that this would be a given in a family of two ministers, but for me, it was a turning point, given my tendency to wrestle for control rather than surrender to blind faith.

In the hospital, the hardest part for me was not being able to be with Brady. I wasn't able to leave my room, and he wasn't able to leave the nursery because he was hooked up to multiple machines. While John was able to run interference, bringing me pictures and videos, I didn't have the opportunity to hold my firstborn until midnight, six hours after his birth. I've felt no greater disconnection than the inability to hold the child that I had carried for nine months. I'll never forget the communion of holding him for the first time. His pediatrician snuck him in for a brief visit after I had broken down hours earlier at her strict warnings that Brady could not leave the nursery. Brady was so calm and observant, staring with those milky new eyes, accepting us. He was so tiny, and yet our lives suddenly felt so big. He felt solid, and we felt complete and whole. He was a miracle, opening my eyes and heart to the wonder of God's creation. It was a holy moment, and John and I both got choked up as we prayed our thanks to God. There was so much longing and fear and hope and love in my heart, so much waiting to be realized. My heart was already growing, but more growth was in store.

I have always been one to hold on tightly—to my plans, to my control, to my own vision of how I expect God to work. Through our new journey with Brady, I slowly began to learn the hard lessons of surrendering my own will and trusting God to work in God's own ways and—even more diffi-cult—in God's own time. Until this point, my faith journey had been much about *my* plans for how God would use me. As a perfectionist with a type-A personality, I relished being in control, believing that if I worked hard enough, I could do everything (and have God's blessing while accomplishing it all). My foundation was built on my own self-confidence. Although I professed faith in God and ministered in God's name, I relied on my own strength and found that I had less and less to pull from. My ministry with at-risk youth in a residential group home was draining and showed little visible signs of success. I was quickly approaching burnout. Now I was also faced with the unexpected medical concerns of my baby and wondered anx-iously how I would juggle caring for him while also living out my calling.

As I am a bit (*ahem*) hardheaded, lessons were not easily learned for me. After returning home from the hospital with our new little one, life took on a new rhythm, one that often sounded of frustration. I beat my head on the wall time and time again (sometimes literally) as I reached roadblock after roadblock. We enrolled Brady in the day care of the church where my husband worked (free childcare, and John was there to oversee it), only to have to pull him out at his doctor's orders when Brady's frequent illnesses kept him from growing as he should. I put a Pack 'n Play in my office, think-ing Brady could snooze the day away while I worked, only to learn that he had other plans and my coworkers had other opinions on the matter.

I struggled each day with breastfeeding: visiting the lactation consultants multiple times a week, pumping milk almost hourly, and taking handfuls of herbal supplements, only to have a lactation consultant gently hand me a bottle of formula for my starving child and tell me that even she wouldn't have worked so hard to succeed. Feeding and sleeping battles continued and led us to our breaking point time and time again, and I expressed my anger and tiredness and frustration to God relentlessly. Instead of seeking God's peace or guidance, however, I continued to read all the books and blogs (that just made me feel more incompetent) and to try and try and try.

Two years after Brady's debut, our daughter, Maryn, was born healthy, but through another dramatic and scary emergency C-section delivery. I experienced post-partum depression that, combined with my husband's unexpected dismissal from his church position and my own burnout at work, brought me to my lowest point. The darkness seemed to engulf me. I felt overwhelmed by the weight of juggling the new reality of supplying the demands of two children while anxiously contemplating our financial and vocational futures. As our babies cried, my delivery scars seared with pain, another reminder of my brokenness.

I prayed earnestly in those days, asking God for something, anything: either an assurance that I was where God wanted me to be or a vision of a new plan. I prayed for peace, for patience, for strength, for our family and for our jobs. I prayed into the silence and numbly went through the motions, feeling unsettled and yet resigned. But for the first time, perhaps, I began to truly accept that so much of my life was out of my control. And instead of that bringing fear as I would have expected, it actually began to soothe my anxiety.

I guess that's the gift of hitting bottom—there's nowhere to go but up. I had to surrender my expectations, understanding that there was freedom in letting go. The greatest failure was holding on to my old patterns, behaviors, and attitudes that were not beneficial. What was the purpose in working so hard if I couldn't change my situation? Why fight with myself (and others) when I couldn't see the big picture of what God was working in my life? I thought a lot about the exodus story, the forty years the Israelites spent wandering (and complaining) in the desert. Since seminary, one of my favorite passages has been Exodus 13:17-18: "When Pharaoh let the people go, God did not lead them by way of the land of the Philistines, although that was nearer; for God thought, 'If the people face war, they may change their minds and return to Egypt.' So God led the people by the *roundabout* way of the wilderness towards the Red Sea. The Israelites went up out of the land of Egypt prepared for battle" (NRSV, emphasis added).

Due to their own fears, God sought to protect the people, and yet they could not understand at the time that their long journey could be part of God's leading. They went out prepared for battle, uncertain as to what they would face. Likewise, I began reflecting on the lessons I was learning through my own desert wanderings and preparing myself for what might lie ahead. Bit by bit, the clouds started parting. Although it would take a long time for circumstances to change, I felt my own spirit lightening a little, just enough to let me breathe. Each deep breath gave me new perspective on the beauty that God had blessed me with in my family, my faith, and my calling. I stopped searching so hard for a "fix" to the stress that assaulted me and instead tried to see with new eyes, understanding that I already had all I needed. I learned that I couldn't control my children's proclivities (like wanting to be attached to me 24/7) or change their habits (like forgoing naps and waking sporadically through the night). Although we provided healthy meals, it didn't mean they would actually eat them. And regardless of the nurturing and safe environment we provided, we couldn't keep them from getting hurt or sick. So much was out of our control.

Instead of focusing on that lack of control and becoming increasingly frustrated at all my perceived failures, I had to trust that God was working in and through our lives in ways seen and unseen. While I had harshly judged our reality for how it was diverging from the carefully painted picture in my mind, I had to allow God to open my eyes to the beauty God had given me in my family as it was. In surrendering, I freed Brady and Maryn to be who God created them to be, and the results have been delightful, challenging, and inspiring. They have taught me so much about simple joy and living in the moment, about living with gratitude and passion. As I cared for them, I began to understand God's unconditional love in a tangible way as I both gave and received that love.

In the same way, I began to understand God through the heart of a parent. When times of hurt and struggle come, it is not God's intention to harm me (or even to test me), but God is there, guiding me through as I develop faith and strength to persevere. I cannot control all of my circumstances, but I can work on controlling my responses. I can trust God to do the work of changing my heart while I change my attitude, and I can allow these changes to influence my behavior and beliefs. As I began to understand parenthood as a long journey of letting go, I could see the connections to my faith and calling.

Just as parenthood had not turned out to be the rosy picture I had painted in my mind, my career and calling had not followed my well-laid plans. Both, however, became even more beautiful and miraculous to me when I was able to let go of my preconceived ideas, plans, and need for control, and instead see how God had guided me (in spite of me). While I struggled and fought, demanding my own way, God had quietly and slowly led me on a roundabout journey designed, I believe, to grow my faith and trust in God's provision.

When my lifelong plan to be a medical researcher did not pan out upon college graduation (because I learned that I was ill-suited for research), God gently guided me toward a volunteer ministry position that captured my heart. This led me to seminary, where I discovered a community of friends and supporters, including the man who would become my husband. Jobs opened for us, fed us and taught us for a while, and then dissolved when there were new lessons to learn and new places and people to serve. Although those were trying and difficult times, they are the points of my journey when I saw the most growth and felt the hand of God leading on, still, through the desert. They are the times when God held us and healed our hurts, just as we lovingly hold and comfort our children.

Letting go, in ministry and motherhood, will be my lifelong struggle. I had another taste of it last fall, as our whole family gathered at the bus stop to send Brady off to kindergarten. He was literally bouncing with excitement, ready for his new adventure. The bus came, and he ran to it, climbing the steps that looked impossibly big compared with his small size. I wanted to snatch my baby back up and protect him from a world that can be scary, intimidating, and cruel. But his smile was so bright and his wave so eager that love and pride bubbled up in my heart as tears came to my eyes. As I sent my first baby off, Maryn's arms encircled my neck. I held her close and felt a wave of gratitude for the gifts I had been given. Sometimes it's time to let go, but other times we have the joy of holding on and being held. It seems that Brady, Maryn, and God still have much to teach me on this journey to the Promised Land.

———◆———

*Rev. **Jenny Frazier Call** is an ordained Baptist minister serving as university chaplain at Hollins University in Roanoke, Virginia. A graduate of the College of William and Mary and the Baptist Theological Seminary at Richmond, she learns the most from her precocious children, Brady (6) and Maryn (4). She couldn't juggle it all without the loving support of her husband, John.*

CHAPTER 5

THEY, SHE, AND THOU ART WITH ME

Stephanie Little Coyne

I

I don't remember where I first heard the idea that babies and people near death were closer to the Spirit of God than others. I think that I shrugged off the idea, probably because I had one of those "my theology is intellectually superior to yours" moments.

Being both a hospice chaplain and a new mom, I find that my current life situation has provided me a palpable plane for proving that idea.

I have struggled lately with my line of work. The energy that is required to make a hospice visit has become both a lot harder to muster up and a lot harder to maintain. The energy required to maintain a relationship with God has also become difficult.

A few weeks ago, I visited yet one more poor soul, about seventy years old, neither breathing nor eating on his own. And then I looked to his roommate, about thirty years old and in the same condition.

In those moments, I offered a plea: *I cannot see one more person like this. I can't do this anymore. God, let me pray to you—but what words can I use? I have none. I have no concentration, no course of connectivity.*

I left, hands stuffed in my pockets, ashamed of my tears. I had the overwhelming feeling that I would no longer be able to do what I felt, and feel, called to do. I wanted to be able to reach out and touch my patient—to somehow communicate to him that I was there for him; I wanted to help bridge the gap between human and divine and let him know that he was loved by both. But I could not. I was frozen and unable.

The next day, I set out again to another patient's home, curious as to whether the long drive into the Bayou would help with my chaplain's block. There, I met with an elderly woman and her family. The visit went well and I left, an adequate chaplain; still, I felt as though my words were garbled and jumbled and late arriving.

On to another patient . . . *breathe in.*

She grabbed my hands before I offered them. Her nails dug into my skin, and I was certain a stream of blood was going to run down into my gray sleeve. Her legally blind eyes looked deeply into mine. "Aren't you a sweet thing," she said without consideration. Her affection stung and cut deeper than her nails.

We talked of dying and heaven and peace. She was clear but repetitive. And then, she looked again at me and spoke: "You're going to make it. There will be rough waters and smooth waters, but God will always be with you."

Really? Had God granted me the gift of turning tables again? Who was the chaplain and who was the patient? Who was the blind one and who could see perfectly?

My tears echoed hers, though I'm not sure why she was crying.

As quickly as her clarity came, it went, and we revisited the memories of her husband, dog, and children.

God, let me discover the message behind this current scatteredness and strug-gle. Push my hands toward the hurt and the hurting and then let me retrieve them with the feeling that they are washed and clean. Lend me the grace to keep course towards your call, and the awakening and the recognition every time I replace your voice with another's. Yours is the one I wish to hear.

II

Many of my patients have some form of dementia. Watching a family wander dementia's dark corridors together is a hard part of the job though it's not as hard as living daily with the darkness. I get to come and go. In the midst of the confusion and repetition, a patient will catch me off guard and say something enlightening with great clarity.

An eighty-nine-year-old woman, stuck in time, not remembering much past 1960, asks me the same questions over and over every time I visit: Where were you born? What year are you in school? Do you live nearby? She tells me the same stories each time I visit too, generally with the same scenes, new remembrances causing only minor variations. She will try to gain some traction in her thoughts by reading any and all words in front of her. During a past visit, she tried to keep up with the words in TV commercials as they moved by quickly. She read out loud the words she caught up with and desperately tried to make sense of them.

Somewhere in this revolving world, she started to shake her head back and forth and say, "It just goes around and around, I don't know what it's about. But I'm glad to be a part of it all. You know?"

I have struggled as a mother with weaning my Annie, in part, I think, because I have not been able to see what the end of the stage looks like. Physical signs occur during this stage that let you know you are going through something, but there is no way of either anticipating or controlling those signs. Throwing the emotional pieces of angst and relief into the Tumbler of No Control makes the cycle, and therefore the stage, seem never-ending.

I recognize this truth: weaning is the last step of physical detachment; the baby was conceived, carried, birthed, and nursed. The end of this journey is only the beginning of the baby's gradual move towards an independent life. Even though the process towards independence is natural and healthy, the parent will struggle to relinquish those ties.

In the humid dusk of a day, Annie and I filled up several empty Frappuccino bottles with dirt and planted some staple herbs in each one, creating our windowsill garden. Sweaty, buggy, and sandy, we headed straight for the shower after we finished. She loves water, no matter its form, even if her face gets wet.

As we rinsed off, she suddenly became still in my arms and placed her face in the crook of my neck. Not since she was just a few days old had she settled down enough to do that for long; she loves to move too much. And of course, the water from the shower was no longer the only source of water on my face. I entered into a full-blown messy cry, and she picked up her head and looked into my wet eyes. Her brow showed puzzlement and she searched for a solution in her seven-month-old resource library. I tried to explain it to her—"Mama loves you so much and she doesn't always have the capacity to deal with it well." I guess that my thirty-two-year-old resource library didn't have an answer either.

She put her head back on my shoulder and fell asleep within a few seconds. I stood there in the cleansing water with my cleansing tears, enjoying the moment, needing the moment, and thanking the Creator for giving me some solace. Peace greatly slows the Tumbler of No Control to a much more manageable pace.

The water from the shower began to lose its warmth, and I was forced to leave the moment behind; however, I stepped out feeling consoled, knowing that, guided and led by Peace, I had discovered the end of this part of the journey.

I know that emotions are circular and that any moment an overwhelming flood may come. I may find that I cannot keep up, that I may struggle for traction, that I may be puzzled and in search of some answers.

Yet I'm glad to be a part of it all.

III

My husband and I, both people who generally think more than we say, somehow created a chatterbox. Annie combines varying phonetic sounds with varying facial expressions and varying volumes. She often gets her hands involved too. The conversation tone can change quickly—she chewed out her stuffed monkey one day though we were not privy to his sudden fault.

She will look at you intently, stretching her arm out, and orate better than any TV evangelist. That little arm reaches high, but thanks to some creative design, only baby-arm high. There's no telling what she would reach if her arms were the same proportions as an adult's arms.

Sometimes I think that I know exactly what she is saying, and then other times I have no idea. I think she thinks the same thing of me. She laughs when I say "no." I hope this is not a sign of things to come. When she recognizes a word or a song, a broad smile appears, even a laugh. Her body lights up, and I'm sure that mine does too. We have expanded our points of connection.

One of my patients is not old; at any rate, he is too young to be in his medical state. He is unable to talk loudly and some days cannot push out a whisper. I knew this going into our first visit, but I still felt completely inadequate during our interaction.

I gave my name and explained my role. I don't always ask, but this time I did ask if I might pray for him. His eyes looked into mine and he nodded. I prayed. I then asked if he needed anything else. He began to mouth words, and I tried to focus all my listening ability on his whisper. I couldn't understand. Trying to focus even harder, with my eyes on his lips, I tried again. Still nothing. I began looking around the room. "Water?" No. "Do you want your head up?" No. "TV off? Up louder?" No. Around the room I went, and I could not find the right object.

Finally, I looked at the windowsill. An open Bible lay in plain view.

I asked, "The Bible?" Yes. Relieved for a "yes," but annoyed at myself for not realizing his wishes sooner, I brought it to him. "Do you want me to read to you?" He nodded. It was open to Psalm 23, and I asked if he wanted to hear that passage. He nodded again. My eyes already cloudy, I started, "The Lord is my shepherd . . . ." I had to stop in the middle of "He restoreth my soul," because my tears were loudly interrupting my speech. A deep breath and apology later, I continued through the end.

What beautiful poetry, what perfect truth. *Thou art with this man.*

Sometimes, when I am gifted to do the holiest parts of my job, the emotion of it catches up with me. In this scene, the communication points were three—God, patient, chaplain. This man lay there, in a state that tests my theology, and he wanted me to act out my role; he wanted me to bring God closer to his side. What else does that gift bring but tears?

In addition to being gifted in the role of chaplain, I too am gifted with the role of mother. I have faith that during our scenes of happiness and our scenes of hurting, God will join in with Annie and me, whatever our emotions may be. The Creator is active, always by the side of the creation, constantly establishing communication points. What else does that gift bring but joy?

Human connection, especially when it comes from love, is a gift, but a gift largely ignored until it is hard to attain. My hope, and I envision it as so, is that the Creator lights up and is filled with joy when all of creation shares the active gift of love with each other. What else does that gift bring but hope?

My confession is this: I don't believe that God has ever taken a break from me, though I am certain that I have had many days of disconnect from God. I would understand it, though, if God did need a Sabbath. I am frustrating, stubborn, egotistical, unfaithful—trying in a lot of ways. But God is always there to hear my confession and to be a source of renewal.

My prayer for my patients is that they find a place of peace, in the green grass or beside the still waters.

Last night, as I rocked my baby to sleep, I thought through what I wanted my prayer for her to be. The prayer is the same—I want her to have peace. If she finds herself in a place of unrest, I want her to be led by the Shepherd back to that place of sanctity and quiet sanctuary.

Thou art with her.
Thou art with this chaplain and this mother.
Thou art with me, bless my soul. Amen.

Stephanie Little Coyne, *originally from Athens, Georgia, lives in New Orleans, Louisiana, with her husband, Jesse; daughter, Annie; and son, Logan. She is a graduate of the University of Georgia (BA, English) and McAfee School of Theology (MDiv). She has worked as a hospice chaplain since 2005. She also serves as the Minister to Children, Youth, and Families at St. Charles Avenue Baptist Church. Her blog, "A Redhead's Revelations," looks at the parallels between chaplaincy, parenthood, literature, and theology.*

CHAPTER 6

MINISTRY, MOTHERHOOD, AND MESSES

Griselda Escobar

On March 23, my son Elijah was born. I was twenty-six years old, married for a little over a year, and a month away from finishing my Bachelor's degree in Biblical and Theological Studies. I was young when I first felt called to ministry and in my mid-teens when I first preached at my home church. So by the time I was twenty-six, I was ready to get to work or continue school.

But when Elijah was born, everything changed. I stayed home with him for two and a half years. Part of me wanted to get to work and began to wonder if that would be an option for me anymore. I had to work through my desire to stay home *and* to do pastoral ministry. Today there are days when my husband reminds me how much I desired to be engaged in ministry work. I still strongly desire it.

I am the oldest of my parents' five children. I was born in Mexico and moved to the United States when I was eight years old. My father is a pastor and has served in ministry since before I was born. My mother is a pastor's daughter and was involved in ministry since her teens. She loves the church and married my dad knowing that they would serve in ministry together. Like me, my mother felt called to ministry at a very young age. She served in the children's department from her early teenage years. She saw her mother as a pastor's wife and knew that she would support her husband's ministry—and that being a good mother would be important to my father's ministry. This part of my cultural and religious background has shaped the way I understand and do ministry and motherhood today.

The community where I grew up had clear roles for both motherhood and pastoral ministry. A mother is feminine, passive, helpful, forgiving, and selfless. She is dependent on her husband, supportive of him, and puts others' needs before her own. She always has an ordered and clean house, and her children are always well dressed and well behaved. The work of housekeeping and child rearing come naturally to her and is always done appropriately.

Unlike women, men in this community are allowed mistakes in these areas, especially in housekeeping and child rearing, because these belong to the mother's role. A woman is expected to prepare for motherhood for a long time. I find this similar to the role imposed on pastors by many churches. The pastor is available, helpful, selfless, spiritually above the congregation, and has the right words to say and the needed advice to give, with success measured by outcomes.

Both motherhood and the pastorate have characteristics that are good for all people to have and are affirmed by Christianity. But when people expect perfection, that expectation becomes oppressive. In life, these characteristics do not always appear when needed and are not always lived out appropriately. Life is at times messy: we suffer unexpected events, make mistakes, and are affected by others' mistakes. It is in the mess that I find myself experiencing the grace of God upon my life and the lives of others. This is the grace I saw working through my mother in the many different roles she served.

Throughout our childhood, my mother cared for five children, served the church without pay, and, for some time, worked a part-time job outside the home. Many of the memories from my childhood include riding in the car after she picked us up from school. She had many things to do and could not leave us at home without her. When we finally got home, she made dinner in what seemed like a few minutes and sent us all to bed while she made sure my dad was ready for the next day. I still remember the noise, sleeping in the car, and the amount of laundry she had to do. At different times, my brother, sister, and father were hospitalized, we were financially unstable, and my father spent much of his time in ministry. I saw my mother struggle, cry, and work hard at fulfilling the roles others imposed on her— and at times the congregation criticized her for not fulfilling those expectations. I saw God use my mother in a special way, and I am thankful she showed me a different way to be minister and mother.

God placed two callings upon my mother's life: one to serve in ministry and the other to be a mother. She answered both callings, as do many pastors. In serving both, she did not always fulfill the expectations for both roles, but she chose to close her ears to the criticism and continue serving God through ministry and motherhood. When I see the blessing she has been to others in ministry, I realize the value of sharing the people God places in our lives *and* the value of sacrificing family time for the well-being of another. I have also been blessed by my mother's sacrifice of placing our needs before hers—just as God placed my needs before anything else (Philippians 2).

Through my mother's commitment to our family and to ministry, I better understand the relationship between Jesus and his Father and the meaning of a church family. I have experienced freedom because of her. I will not fulfill the role of a pastor, according to some, and I do not fulfill every role of a mother, according to others, but this does not change the fact that I am a pastor *and* I am a mother.

In my ministry experience, I had the opportunity to meet a wonderful family one Monday morning at work. I was told that the family arrived on Saturday evening with their daughter, who was very sick. The family was not in the unit I cover in the hospital, but they spoke only Spanish, and I was the only Spanish-speaking chaplain. The couple has four daughters between the ages of seven and twenty. Their eighteen-year-old daughter was in the intensive care unit on a breathing machine because she could no longer breathe on her own and was not doing well. I met the patient, who was conscious, and her parents, who were obviously very worried. I accompanied the family when the doctor told them that their daughter appeared to have a rare lung cancer that had rapidly spread to her bones and blood system. The cancer had also reached her left leg and ovaries. He offered chemotherapy, but not to save her or heal her from the cancer. It was too late. He offered it to try buying their daughter some time for them to spend with her before she died.

I cannot tell you what they were feeling or thinking. I do not know how I would be if I was told something like that about my son. But I know exactly what I was feeling as the chaplain: I felt inadequate, completely and utterly unable to say anything. I went through different things that I could say to bring comfort or courage, but there was nothing. I sat with the patient's parents in the conference room and held their hands as we cried. During that week, a critical care doctor talked to me about the possibility of discussing comfort care with the parents and providing her a better quality of life at the end rather than continuing aggressive treatment.

With this in mind, I approached the parents to see how they would feel about comfort care. This was difficult to do because I understood from the doctor that comfort care was more humane, but I felt angry that I had to ask the parents for such a decision. I thought of my cousin who died at sixteen of cancer. I thought of my son and how I would feel. I thought of their daughter and the life they had dreamed for her. When I mentioned the possibility of comfort care, the patient's father asked me, "Would you move her to comfort care if she was your daughter?" The mother was with him, and with tears in her eyes she looked at me for my response. With a sinking heart I told them that I did not know.

For the next month, I sat with this couple and their daughters, including the patient, and listened to their pain, frustration, anger, guilt, memories, and hope in the midst of this crisis. I was left without words most of the time, but I provided my support to them in any decision they made. After a twenty-four-hour on-call duty shift, I was told the patient was dying. I stayed with the family and saw her mother lie on the bed with her and felt her father trembling when I hugged him as we waited. I felt extremely tired, but I could not imagine how they felt after many sleepless nights in a hospital room trying to rest on a reclining chair.

The medical team was hurting to see this young girl die and not be able to do anything for her. I saw ministry needs for the parents, the extended family who had arrived, and the medical staff. I felt overwhelmed. We were all a mess.

Their daughter died that afternoon, a little over a month after arriving at the hospital. Progress was made at times, but she continually declined throughout her treatment. I do not know if comfort care would have prolonged or shortened her life span, but I do know that her parents did what they felt necessary, and I supported them through it.

When I think back on what happened, I see Jesus. As I sat in the room with the patient and her parents into the late hours of the night when I was on call, I sat with Jesus. As I held the patient's hand or her mother's, I held the hand of Christ. As I cried with the family and staff when she died, I cried with a loving God who suffered along with them through the entire process. At the same time that I sat there, intently listening and providing my presence and touch, they experienced the presence of God by their side.

The muddled feelings that come with ministry at times also come with motherhood. Children hear from their parents the good news of God, and the parents then become the children's first image of God. We are the first to teach our children forgiveness, unconditional love, justice, mercy, and grace. Our children will begin to experience God through the lenses that we have placed on them. This feels like a lot of responsibility. My ministry experience influences my motherhood experience and vice versa.

In getting to know my son, I am also getting to know God in very special ways. I see God in the constant forgiving and sincere love of a child. I see God in my son's creativity, faith, and confidence to be himself. I embody God's presence for my son in building his trust, because he knows that every time he calls I will respond. He knows that I will always forgive him; he knows that nothing can change my love for him. He experiences God's forgiveness and grace as he experiences mine and learns to accept forgiveness as he sees me accept forgiveness from God and others, including himself.

My last on-call duty experience was busy. I slept a total of about four hours (which is really good for call duty), but I had emotionally difficult situations and felt emotionally and physically drained. I had recently started a new job that would become my full-time job when I finished clinical pastoral education. When I left the hospital after call duty, I went home, took a shower, and headed to my new job. After another full day of work, my husband and I stopped at church to counsel a couple. My son had fallen asleep by then, and he took a nap on a church bench while my husband and I ministered to the couple.

It was late by the time we arrived home, and Elijah was desperate to spend time with me. I only spent a few minutes at bedtime with him that night because he fell asleep after his shower and bedtime story. I was lying in his bed and began to cry because I had not spent time with him for two days. All I could think was that tomorrow had to be all about him.

I see God's grace in my strong desire to be a good mother and how that is revealed in the daily reality of motherhood. My husband is a strong support for me, and I strongly support him in his ministry. We will continue to experience chaos at times, but God's grace will continue to carry us through.

Writing this essay has been difficult. As I came close to finishing this year of clinical pastoral education, my husband and I decided to have a second child. We prayed about our decision only to realize later that pregnancy is no longer a possibility for us. This is difficult to talk about because it is very recent and painful. My desire to go through the wonderful and horrible nine months, the miracle of feeling a child growing in me, was suddenly snatched away, and it hurt.

My husband and I have gone through the decision-making process, and I had to endure surgery and, although it is not complete, physical recuperation. During the time I wrote this essay, the decision to adopt was made—and changed. The desire to adopt had been in my heart long before I knew this would happen, but after my surgery it became urgent. I began looking for a bigger place to live, went through a list of adoption agencies and picked one, and began to share with close friends that we were adopting. I thought and dreamt of having another child at home as soon as possible.

Through conversation with a friend regarding this essay, I began to pay attention to my rush. I realized I was trying to clean up the mess of my loss. I still want to adopt. I am just slowing down to allow God's grace to continue to manifest in my life as a ministering mother.

When I first saw the e-mail inviting me to write this essay, all I could do was think about the loss I was experiencing of a future story I had longed to be a part of. As I have thought through my writing, I have seen God's companionship through this entire process. God has provided detail after detail through people all around us demonstrating care for us, including this essay. God's grace has held me through my messy feelings of anger, sadness, discouragement, and inadequacy. God has loved on me and walked the journey with me as I do with my patients, parishioners, and son. My inability to give birth to another child does not change my image as mother for Elijah or for another child that might come into our lives in the future through adoption.

The roles that I learned as a child of motherhood and ministry look very different from the roles I fulfill now as mother and minister. But I am proud of the ministering mother I am. Yes, it is messy. But God is great at working with messy.

----●◆●----

*Rev. **Griselda Escobar*** *is a chaplain for the Hospice of East Texas in Tyler. She has a BA in Biblical and Theological Studies from the Baptist University of the Americas, an MDiv from Logsdon Seminary, and did Clinical Pastoral Education at Trinity Mother Frances Hospital. Griselda is a recipient of the Addie Davis Award from Baptist Women in Ministry for leadership in Pastoral Care. She is married to Allan Escobar, and they have a six-year-old son named Elijah.*

CHAPTER 7

A TIME FOR EVERY PURPOSE

Nicole Finkelstein-Blair

I've heard that there are little girls who spend their childhoods cuddling dolls and dreaming of the day they'll be grown-ups with babies of their own.

I was not one of those girls. The beloved Christmas presents of my childhood were not lifelike plastic babies but books and a typewriter. Instead of playing house, I played school and newspaper. In my memory album, where I filled in the blank of "what I want to be when I grow up," my beginner's handwriting says that I wanted to be a doctor, a lawyer, a writer, and/or a missionary. Maybe marriage and children were a given; maybe I just assumed they'd be in there somewhere, but all the way through school, my daydreams were flooded with images of power suits, international travel, and my name on the dust jackets of brilliant books. There was no space in that dream to think too much about spouse or house or babies.

In college, I began to see how the foundations of my faith might be fertile ground for my vocation. I also met my husband, and our individual calls to ministry seemed to dovetail as we each went on to seminary and ordination. We never decided not to have children, but we didn't dream of it either until several years later when—much to our amazement—it suddenly seemed to be The Right Time.

And time has never been the same since.

A Season for Everything

The day my first child was born, my instruments for counting time changed.

As a college student and seminarian, I measured time by semesters, marked with essay deadlines and punctuated by final exam schedules. Later, as a minister and worship leader, I measured time by the lectionary, marked with liturgical colors and punctuated by Advent wreaths and Communion tables.

But then—the delivery room. Minutes measured by time between contractions. Hours versus centimeters. Seconds between the monitor's bleeps. The waiting stillness before that first newborn wail.

On that maternity ward in the middle of a September night, I became a mother, and the only time that counted was now.

"There is an appointed time for everything," wrote the Teacher in the book of Ecclesiastes. For the student, there is a time to study and a time to be tested, a time to read the experts and a time to write down what you think you know. For the liturgist, there is a time to light candles and a time to extinguish them, a time to wear purple and a time to wear green. For every book, every lecture, every homily, every prayer—there is a season. You can mark your calendars by them: cram for your finals, plan your sermon series, and schedule your vacations. You can measure the hours, days, semesters, Sundays, Holy Weeks, and not-so-holy weeks. You can count them down as they pass, and you can plan ahead for those that are to come.

For the mother, though, time is counted differently—and time counts differently. The calendar—annual or liturgical—becomes a backdrop to the now: the midnight feedings, the first smiles, the mysterious rashes. The exhilaration and the exhaustion of bringing life to birth and carrying it through the "every days" to come.

Now is the mother's time. We may try to remember it all as we scrapbook the memories and milestones, taking copious notes to record all the wondrous "firsts." We may try to schedule our lives as we fill our calendars with birthday parties and play dates. But for the mother, there is no looking back or planning ahead that outranks this moment, the now. There is a time for holding hands—now. There is a time for wiping tears—now. There is a time for eating your vegetables—now (and, all right, there's also a time for cookies, later . . . but veggies now!). There is a time for comforting bad dreams, for learning ABCs, for rock-paper-scissors, for "Jesus Loves Me." There is also a time for driver's ed, for first loves and first heartbreaks, for navigating the hard questions of faith and self. There is a time for all these, and for the mother that time is—always—now.

So we learn to count time differently. No clock or calendar is adequate, so we find new ways to measure, as best we can, as mothers have always done: not by the clock's ticking hands or the calendar's turning pages, but by each breath, each smile, each step, each word, each tear. We mark the nows by treasuring them, by treasuring all these times and seasons, and by holding them close. By pondering them in our hearts. As mothers have always done.

A Time for Every Purpose

"Treasuring this moment" is a spiritual discipline that tends to elude me. As long as I can remember, I've been more interested in the next; I've been future-oriented, always busily planning ahead for the next activity, project, event, holiday. Pregnancy was a nine-month-long festival of "what's next?" jam-packed with an invigorating regimen of list making, calendar updating, appointment scheduling, nursery organizing.

But when my son was born, I decided (against every natural impulse) that I would live in the moments with him. I knew I would have to restrain the planner in my head and choose again and again throughout his babyhood not to jump ahead mentally toward the future. Instead, I'd try to be fully with him in each stage of his life. I'd choose not to daydream about the time he'd sleep through the night, or say his first word, or read Harry Potter for the first time. I'd choose to stay right there with him for every diaper change and spit-up session, every re-rereading of Humpty Dumpty, every sappy episode of the innocuous purple dinosaur. I'd choose again and again to let the future stay in the future, and keep myself with my son in the now.

It's now eight years later, and we've added another little boy; we've relocated four times in our life as a military family; we've been congregants in four different churches. Eight years, and I am still practicing, still choosing to be here—and even more, to be now—with the kids and their sticky faces, wrestling matches, Lego messes, clumsy cuddles, bedtime prayers.

"There is a time for every occupation under heaven," wrote the Teacher, and as a mother I wonder: Does there really have to be a time for dirty diapers and potty training? For sibling rivalries? For missed-nap meltdowns? For picky eating? For school bullies? Is there really a time for time outs and for temper tantrums? For hurt feelings and broken hearts? For slamming doors and sullen moods?

The answer, I think, is yes.

Yes, there is a time for all those things, just as surely as there is a time for tickle fights and Looney Toons marathons, a time for Sunday school popsicle-stick crafts, a time for "Carry me!" and a time for "I do it myself!"

For all these there is a time, and even a purpose under heaven. For our children, these are the occupations of growing up. My boys have the task of finding their way in the world, learning to navigate self and others, faith and fears. But the challenging work and rollicking laughter of child time isn't only for the kids' benefit; all these occupations of childhood are also shaping me as a mother. By being in time with my children, walking alongside them and growing together with them, I am changing just as surely as they are.

It can only happen in the moments, though. Before motherhood, I would have made a plan, set goals, determined the steps to get where I needed to go and to become who I needed to be. I had a theological understanding of God's Presence and a theoretical belief in being present myself, but my real confidence was in my ability to see the big picture of the pathway and to puzzle out how to move forward.

But when I watch my children and let them teach me how to grow, I realize that growing happens in the moments, in all the many times of life. It doesn't happen because I set a goal or made a plan (much to my frustration!). It happens because I am here and because I am human, and because being human means growing inches and gaining pounds, learning new words and ways of relating, discovering that I will stumble and fall but that I can also ease my way up again, accepting that the world might not look like I'd expected but that there is a place for me in it.

A Time to Embrace

Yes, I've always tended to be future-oriented. I love the promise of possibility, envisioning what awaits; I love the feeling of being drawn ahead, pulled forward into the journey's next steps. I love tending goals and drawing up plans. I love the sense of being called toward something.

There was a time—when I was a seminarian, and then a newly ordained minister—when that call seemed clear. There were goals to meet and plans to make: a degree program, an internship, an ordination, a ministry position. I'd undergone the standard inventories for discerning my gifts, had trusted mentors encouraging me, felt confident that I was being prepared for a certain path, and was ready and anxious to step forward into that vocation.

Looking back, it seems those days of preparation for ministry were, in their way, days of great pregnancy. I felt deeply aware of a new kind of life that was taking shape in me, cells of experience and education and giftedness and calling, multiplying exponentially and clustering together into a wondrously made new creation: the Pastor. I eagerly anticipated the birth of that future; I showered it with office supplies and reference books, outfitted it with stoles in every color, scheduled it for youth camps and committee meetings.

This is not the future I was expecting.

A stay-at-home mom, with a job description for which none of my education has prepared me: gatherer of stuffed animals, dinner-table liturgist, evangelist for personal hygiene, sibling-relations counselor.

I am now eight years into this season of the vocation of motherhood, and it is a far cry from the future I once felt summoning me forward. Living the moments with my children, I try to give them grace as I remember that they are growing into some things, outgrowing others, going through phases (some of which are not fun!), and gradually becoming the people God is already calling them to be. Even as I choose to be with them in their now, I'm also slowly learning to be here, and to be now, with myself. I'm learning to give myself grace as I remember that I too am growing and outgrowing, going through some not-fun phases, and gradually becoming the person God is still calling me to be. I'm hopeful that with practice I will ever more fully believe that there truly is a time to every purpose under heaven, because if I can believe that there's a time for every silly song and every lullaby, a time for every milk spill and every cookie-crusted face, then maybe I can also believe that there is a time—and a purpose—for me.

Some days, though, I have to wonder.

There are days when all the goals and plans that once beckoned, all the possibilities of the pastoral vocation I once dreamed, seem dim, distant. The call still hums along underneath my days, but it is muted, and that pulling-forward, summoning future that has always driven me seems to have stilled. Perhaps I've subdued it for now, the way I try to hush (for now) the day-dreams of sitting down with my sons to read about The Boy Who Lived. Maybe the Voice is simply quieter than the other sounds of my life, difficult to hear behind the clamor of little-boy noises. Maybe the call has been transformed so dramatically that I need to learn to listen to it differently. Maybe I have been transformed so dramatically that I must learn to hear differently.

It can be a difficult time to embrace. But I'm learning to live now instead of always next. I'm learning to see the small steps of growth as occupations that are full of purpose. And I'm also learning, as a mother, how to open my arms and pull my dreams into my lap . . . especially the two sticky, noisy, bed-headed dreams I never knew I had until I had them. So I can embrace these days and years the way I embrace my children: letting go of the disappointments, lifting up hopes for their becoming, but finally just loving them for what they are. I can embrace them with concern because I know the world can be scary; I can embrace them with fierceness, trying to lend them strength because I know that they will sometimes be broken. I can embrace them with boundless joy, with unspeakable thanksgiving for their goodness. And I can even embrace my dreams with tears in my eyes, willing to let them go.

Rev. Nicole Finkelstein-Blair became a US Navy spouse in 2000, graduated from Central Baptist Theological Seminary and was ordained in 2001, and became "Mom!" in 2004. She finds ministry wherever the military and motherhood lead: in four states and two countries (so far), as a parishioner and a pulpit-supplier, as a sometime blogger and devotional writer, and at countless dinner tables and bedtimes. She's enjoying "now" and looking forward to what's next.

CHAPTER 8

OTHER PEOPLE'S CHILDREN: SALOME AND MOTHERHOOD

Jenny Folmar

It was late on a Tuesday afternoon. Several teenagers in my office sprawled out on a forty-year-old love seat, their feet propped on the cheap coffee table I bought for that purpose. For them to be there in the middle of the week, I am sure that we were either discussing drama or they were pitching their latest idea for a youth outing.

Either way, my door was open when a friend popped in, holding her half-awake daughter. She asked if I could watch her little one for an hour while she was in a meeting. Of course I could! I took Ellie, a toddler, from her mom and sat back down behind my desk with the child in my lap. Ellie looked around the room at the teenagers and then curled up against me and fell back asleep. What easy babysitting! She settled into heavy breathing in a matter of seconds. It was possible to rock her and go back to the conversation the young people and I were having before the interruption. I rubbed Ellie's back and asked what we were talking about. The teenagers just looked at me.

It was as if I had sprouted a tail and grown wings. They gawked in awkward silence. Finally, one asked, "Are you her godmother?"

I was both flattered and confused. "No, I just babysit her a lot. Why?"

All three youth stared quizzically. Clearly, the side of me that rocked young children was alien to them. They regularly heard me say things like, "I am not your mother!" in the context of my unwillingness to clean after them or pamper them.

Finally, one of the girls asked if I wanted to be a mom. I let them know that I do want children one day, but that the husband who usually comes first is still nowhere to be seen. She paused a second and then said, "Miss Jenny, you should *totally* have kids! You would be a great mom! If you don't find a husband, you should totally adopt. But you can't have kids any time soon. At least, not until I graduate. You aren't allowed to love anyone but us."

A better minister would probably have a verse to quote about God's love and abandonment issues. I just laughed. I realized that I had an office full of other people's children, and the older ones were quickly growing jealous of the toddler in my lap.

Other people's children. I don't remember when I started using this phrase, but I do know that it began as a joke. When looking lovingly on a baby, I will sigh and quietly say, "Wow. I sure love other people's children." It always gets a laugh. The implication is that I am a single, childless minister who loves the freedom to nurture children for an hour or two and then send them home with their parents, who do all the hard work. The phrase became a tool. It succeeds in circumventing any questions about children of my own.

With time, that funny little phrase grew sacred, but not until I began to embrace that part of my calling to ministry. I had to first grow comfortable with being a childless mother figure in the church.

Accepting this part of ministry did not come naturally. I did not have a childhood that included joyful, thriving, childless women. If there were women without children, people spoke about them with a strong dose of sadness, as if they had a terminal disease. I needed to replace those fearful and sad images with new models that offered a bit of hope.

I stumbled upon Mary Salome when my spiritual director encouraged me to find a person of faith to use as an image of inspiration. Out of curiosity, I looked up the saint for my birthday: Mary Salome or simply Salome. *Who?* There was little more than a paragraph available for this person on the Internet. Happily, I read that she was a different Salome than the woman who danced to have John the Baptist beheaded. She grabbed my attention when I learned that she walked with Jesus through his entire life.

In the Bible, Salome is not prominent. She is listed twice in the Gospel of Mark among the women who witnessed Jesus' death and who later encountered an angel at the empty tomb (Salome is named in Mark 15:40 and 16:1). Mark describes the relationship between Jesus and Mary Magdalene, Mary mother of James, and Salome, saying, "These used to follow him and provided for him when he was in Galilee; and there were many other women who had come up with him to Jerusalem" (Mark 15:41, NRSV). The Bible does not give Mary Salome her own story or even a voice, but she is listed as one of the dedicated women who followed and served Jesus.

Early Christian writings, however, are full of her stories and conversations with Jesus. Some claim that Mary Salome was Jesus' aunt. Others claim that she was Jesus' sister or Mary's midwife. In some traditions she is married with children, and in others she is childless (see Richard Bauckham: "Salome the Sister of Jesus, Salome the Disciple of Jesus, and The Secret Gospel of Mark," *Novum testamentum XXXIII 3* [1991]: 245–75).

Our friend, Mary Salome, seems to appear quite often in the early Christian story. Most scholars who study her agree on the following: She was present at Jesus' birth. She remained with Mary and Joseph as they raised Jesus. She followed Jesus through his ministry and witnessed both his crucifixion and resurrection. *The Discourse by Demetrius* describes her this way:

> Now this woman Salome was the first who recognized the Christ, and who worshipped Him, and believed in Him when He came upon the earth, and she did not return to her own house until the day of her death. Whithersoever Christ went to preach, with His mother the Virgin, there she followed Him with His disciples until the day when they crucified Him and [the day of] His holy resurrection. She saw them all, with His mother the Virgin. (E. A. Budge, British Museum, *Miscellaneous Coptic Texts* [London: Printed by the Order of Trustees, no date] 674).

Women of the early church were familiar with Salome. They had a model for what it looked like when a woman committed to caring for someone else's child, who happened to be Jesus Christ. What a gift! Little girls long ago were told stories of their sister in Christ, Salome, who knew Jesus' mother and became one of his disciples.

As I grow more familiar with Salome, I wish that there were T-shirts or blogs that celebrate her ministry. It would be great to have empowering slogans like "Following Jesus like Salome" or "Rockin' Ministry Salome Style" to dissipate some of the extreme awkwardness for female ministers who walk into church doors without a child or a wedding ring.

But we have no bumper stickers or T-shirts. The reality is that Christian communities have a difficult time with childless women. We catch ourselves asking the unfair question that comes to mind when meeting a kind, smart,

childless clergy

loving woman past a certain age. *Why doesn't she have children?* The question itself can open wounds or add to the experience of feeling judged for lack of children.

Perhaps some women wanted children but were not able to conceive. Some might have lost a baby and could not bring themselves to have another. Still others are called to serve God and love others without having children of their own. Many of the latter feel as if they are somehow wrong or broken because they do not feel called to be mothers.

My awareness of this tension grows with each year that passes. I minister in the South, where most women marry and have children in their twenties. As I settle into my mid-thirties, I let myself laugh a bit when someone hears my marital status and age. There is always a flash of panic or pity in their eyes, followed by a change of subject or a comment about someone they heard about who found love in their fifties. Apparently, being thirty-four and single is the same as being fifty-four when you are ministering in the church.

These predictable moments are why I adopted the phrase, "other people's children."

Other people's children. With time, I embraced the life that God gave me, and my sarcastic little quip began to grow sacred. The shift began when I earned my commercial driver's license to drive the church bus. They never told me in seminary that the most humbling and daunting part of ministry is the trust parents give you when allowing you to drive their children through stormy weather on a busy highway. I found myself saying things like, "Well, I spent church money on the more expensive brakes because I am about to drive to Florida with a bus full of other people's children."

The shift continued when I arrived in the emergency room to wide-eyed and frightened college students whose roommate had been victimized the night before. I came with doughnuts and Mountain Dew. I prayed with them and asked the nurses questions that college students do not know to ask. A week later, one of the girls said to me, "Thank you for being there. We were so scared. It was like you were our mom. I've decided that you are kind of like the mom of our college house." Her tone had a genuine ring with a bit of humor in it, both funny and sacred.

 I like to think that Salome would have showed up at the hospital with doughnuts and Mountain Dew. She, after all, was the first Christian to show us how to walk with another woman's son as if he were her own. Her model of ministry is seen every Sunday in the church where women of all ages and situations seamlessly love and nurture children together. At its best, church is a place where children know the love of an entire community of adults.

Where else but in the church can a child receive a smile, a correction, or a comforting embrace from any adult who passes her way? Where else does God grant us the honor of covenanting together to raise and nurture newborn babies in baby dedications? Where else but in our inheritance of saints does a woman witness the birth of a little boy in a manger and decide to spend her life caring for and following him?

Practically, most of my days are spent in an office or car preparing for the few precious hours each week that we have together as a church. I often forget about the mothering nature of ministry until I am in the middle of a situation and find myself loving someone as if they were my own. Those lines between pastoral care and motherhood seem to blur quite often. My ministry is made much more beautiful by the sacred passing moments when I have the honor to love other people's children.

Rev. Jenny Folmar *grew up in Colleyville, Texas. She earned a BA in Communications at Baylor University and then went on to Princeton Theological Seminary, where she earned a MDiv. Jenny currently serves as the Minister to Youth and College at Memorial Baptist Church in Buies Creek, North Carolina. Jenny most enjoys preaching, worship leadership, and late-night conversations with students. She and her dog, Tina Turner, live in Angier, North Carolina.*

CHAPTER 9

ONCE UPON A TIME: THE TALE OF A NOT-SO-WICKED STEPMOTHER

Kerrie Clayton Jordan

Once upon a time, I dreamed of living happily ever after with Prince Charming in a castle filled with love and romance. As I fantasized about finding Mr. Right during my twenty-something years, I still managed to maintain a spirit of adventure—focusing on my career as a woman in ministry, going back to school for my Master of Divinity, traveling the world on mission and educational trips, and waiting (sometimes patiently, sometimes not so patiently) for a husband who would partner with me in ministry. Single life was pretty good most of the time. There was no one or nothing to hold me back from pursuing my dreams. My future fairy tale may or may not have included children—it was something I could've lived with or without. I wasn't sure being a mom was for me, but if Prince Charming wanted children, his wish was my command.

In early 2010, I was swept off my feet by a man named David, a single father of two children: twelve-year-old Walker and four-year-old Hope. As soon as I met David, I knew he was the man I would marry, and his handsome character and desire to serve God enchanted me from the beginning. All good fairy tales must have some kind of conflict, and mine was within. I wasn't sure that I wanted children, after all. What would it be like to raise someone else's? Would they like me? Would they *love* me? Would they hate me? (Stepmothers always get a bad rap in the fairy tales!) What would it be like to have an instant family?

During our year of courtship, a custody battle for the children reared its ugly head when the mother (we'll call her Sharon) physically abused Walker, bloodying his nose in the car. The downward spiral with Sharon continued. Run-ins with social services, drugs, mental illness, incarcerations, relationships with men of criminally recurrent behavior . . . and then her phone calls and supervised visits became less and less.

About three months before I married their dad, Hope and Walker lost all contact with Sharon, and David received primary custody of both children, much to our relief. Not only was I going to deal with being a stepmom but I was also going to have to learn to be the full-time mom to these two kids. They felt rejected and abandoned by the very woman who gave them life. Would I be up for the challenge? Did I even stand a chance of making a difference in their lives? After all, in the usual fairy tales, the stepmother was always villainous and wicked.

And villainous and wicked I am at times. Why? Because I insist on home-cooked family meals around the dinner table without the television on. Because I help their dad enforce a regular bedtime. Because I allow no video games or playtime until homework is finished. I have been resented for having high expectations and standards in place that were never there before. I have been tested to see if my loyalty will remain or if I will just walk away when things get difficult. Sometimes, I am even intentionally pushed away for fear of getting too close, because they know that if they don't love me too much, then it won't hurt as bad if I leave.

One major challenge of being a stepmom is the search for identity. Professionally, I am identified as a minister. Personally, I am not completely mother, but I am not completely childless either. I am expected to act as a mother, but I have never known what it is like to have a child of my own. I never got to experience all the "firsts" of the children I love: their first word, first step, or first Christmas; and I wasn't the first woman to have a child with the man I love. It is tempting to be bitter because I didn't get to experience the full joy of motherhood—bitter toward my husband, my children, and God—and some days I do give in to the grief of knowing I'm not really their mother. How does one even begin to come to terms with the ambiguity of being a mothering stepmother, or to comprehend the identity of being a childless mother-minister?

For now, David and I have decided not to have any more children to add to our family, for various reasons. Because I have no idea how to be a full-time mom, I am more impatient than the average mother who has had years to learn a go-with-the-flow approach to child rearing; and I have a hard time choosing my battles. I often harbor feelings of inadequacy as I wonder if I have the "right" feelings toward my stepchildren who need me to be their mother. And I wonder if I love them less than I would my own biological child, but I will likely never know for sure. Because of my lack of experience in mothering, perhaps I *am* the wicked stepmother because I really don't know *how* to be a mother. After all, it's not like there is a book that I can read about *What to Expect When You're Expecting to Be a Stepmother* or, at the very least, *Stepmothering for Dummies.*

So as every good Christian does, I look to the Bible for help. But there are very few examples of stepparenting in the Bible, and some of those are stretching the definition (Eli to Samuel, Pharaoh's daughter to Moses, Sarah to Ishmael, Mordecai to Esther). If I can't find any guidelines in the Bible, then how can I know what God expects of me as a stepparent? Even some of the world's foremost organizations for the Christian family don't address someone like me: the childless stepparent. In preparation for writing this chapter, I decided to check my church's library, which has two or three shelves devoted to family life, but I only found one book that addressed the stepparent perspective. Come to think of it, I don't know *anyone,* Christian or not, who is in a situation like mine, so I've resorted to joining the "Childless Stepmoms" and "Insta-moms" groups on Facebook for support and advice—often practical, seldom biblically based. What's a stepmom to do?

Stepparenting in the Bible

Having searched for an example of a stepparent in the Scriptures, the best I can come up with is Joseph, the earthly father of Jesus. He was essentially asked to be a stepparent, but we don't know much about his early years as a father. What was his attachment to Jesus like? I am sure he had feelings of inadequacy, just like any first-time parent would, but was there a constant reminder that Joseph wasn't a biological father to Jesus? When Jesus was "lost" in the temple in Jerusalem, being about his Father's business in his Father's house, how did that make Joseph feel? Wasn't he the father, too? Wasn't he the father who was worried sick about the whereabouts of his son while he searched for three long days?

Many times, it's easy to forget that the people in the Bible were real humans, and we are tempted to create a happily-ever-after story. We would like to think that Joseph said everything was okay when he learned where Jesus was and that this was the end of it. Yet how would you feel if your child said, "I was just at church," when you thought they were playing in the backyard? I think that maybe Joseph was upset because Jesus made his parents worry, and then, to top it all off, he couldn't even provide a punishment because Jesus was exactly where he belonged. What if deep down inside he was angry—angry with God in the form of his son, no less—and frustrated because at this moment he felt inadequate and disrespected as a father?

I'm actually a little jealous of Joseph because he had it fairly easy for a stepparent. After all, he was parenting the sinless Son of God, so how hard could it be? And he also got to raise Jesus from the time he was a newborn baby—an innocent, spotless Lamb of God. What about those of us who get a brokenhearted, smart-mouthed, angry teenager for a stepchild? At least Joseph had time to learn patience and to grow in love while he parented the perfect One. I never had that luxury because I jumped headfirst into a situation different from what I had ever known and had to learn to be a wife, mother to a teenager, and mother to a preschooler all at the same time.

As a stepparent, it's important to remember what Joseph likely had to learn: "This is *God's* child." We are but instruments of God's love and care to God's child, and God has entrusted us with great responsibility. In my situation and so many others, the stepparent is asked to be a healing balm to a troubled child's heart. In divorce, death, or absence—in every situation that creates the opportunity for a stepparent—a child is left grieving what they've lost or what they've never known, and a godly stepparent could be the one who steps in and ministers to a hurting, broken family. The other three people who live in my home have been broken and bruised, abandoned and rejected; yet I am called to be the presence of Christ to them through mothering and homemaking.

Trading Ashes for Beauty

Brokenness. It is only out of brokenness that blended families are even possible. When a traditional family unit experiences a death or divorce, no matter the circumstance, there is hurt, anger, disappointment, grief, depression, blame, bitterness, loss, tension, stress, and almost any other emotion on the spectrum—especially for the children. Even if the divorce improves the current health of the relationship, there is a lasting impact on all involved, and brokenness is still there. Broken hearts, broken lives, broken family pieces, and—more often than not—broken children.

My children came to me from a loss that I have never experienced, nor do I hope to experience. I don't know what it is like to suddenly lose a parent or to even have my parents separate. I have never experienced abandonment on the same level as they have. But I *do* know what it's like to be broken, for my heart to be scattered into a thousand jagged pieces and aching from loss, hurt, and disappointment. Everyone experiences a sense of brokenness at some point in our lives, for we live in a broken, imperfect world.

From Job to Jesus to Paul, there are countless passages and people in the Bible where we could find examples of brokenness. The biblical account of the Old Testament Joseph is one that has held the most promise for our family. One of the first devotional times our family spent together (before David and I even married) used portions of Genesis 37–50.

Old Testament Joseph came from a history of brokenness. Joseph was already in a blended family of sorts: Jacob; Jacob's favored wife, Rachel; his other wife, Leah; and his two concubines. Surely the situation became even more complicated when Rachel died in childbirth bearing Joseph's younger brother, creating an opening for a stepmother position. Joseph was also his father's favorite child, making his eleven brothers and one sister jealous, and his ability to interpret dreams didn't make him any more acceptable.

The gift of brotherhood didn't stop the brothers from getting rid of Joseph. They abandoned him, sparing his life but selling him into Egyptian slavery. Joseph: a son without a mother, now without his whole family, a stranger in a foreign land. The story continues with tales of leadership, false accusations, imprisonment, and more dream interpretations. More opportunities for brokenness and remembrances of why he was in Egypt in the first place. It could've ruined Joseph if he had allowed himself to drown in his sea of loss. My children can relate.

Two children abandoned by their mother. A teenager full of anger for the rejection he faces. A four-year-old confused because "mama" doesn't come to see her anymore. Physical, verbal, and emotional abuse. A single dad carrying on and soothing the wounds. Belongings and memories destroyed. A new place to live. Confusion. Hurt. Rejection. Wounded hearts.

Thankfully, we know the rest of the story for Joseph. In Genesis 50 we read of forgiveness and reconciliation with the brothers who wronged him. Because of Joseph's faith in the God of wholeness, brokenness was only part of the journey. If I had to choose a theme verse for my family, it would be Joseph's words in Genesis 50:20 (NLT): "You intended to harm me, but God intended it all for good." The road is often long, the resentment and brokenness in my children's hearts is often turned into frustration toward me, and there is still infinitely more healing to be found in this journey.

I am a stepmom. A broken, sinful, clueless, wannabe mother. Yet I am called to point my children on the road from brokenness to wholeness, to trade in ashes of despair for a crown of beauty. When mothers sometimes harm their children, God can use a stepmother (even if she's a fairy-tale-like evil one at times) to intend it all for good.

The Ministry of Stepmothering

I have often said that one's ministry to his or her family *is* a ministry to the church. How often hurting and broken families look to their church leadership for examples of healthy marriages, family relationships, and encouragement! If we ministers neglect our families, it is most certainly neglecting our calling to ministry. Stepparenting is no different. I've gone from a life focused on a professional ministry career to a life focused on another mother's children. It is ministry in its rawest, most vulnerable form, because the ones who live under my own roof carry a deep scar in their hearts regarding "the other mama" (as my daughter, Hope, calls her biological mother). Sometimes we must act on the ministry of presence while we hold and love the child who cries for their missing parent, reassuring them of our own abiding love for that child. We must remind them that there is a parent who has promised never to leave or forsake. Sometimes, it is silently being the one who absorbs the angry and hurtful resentment the child wants to direct toward an absent (either physically or emotionally) parent. It is being the presence of Christ to a broken world—and a broken home.

It is important for career ministers to remember the unique situation in which our kids are placed by our choices, not theirs. Our job doesn't change, but all of life has changed for our stepchildren. "Regular" kids are all of sudden "preacher's" kids, often looked upon differently by our congregations, with high expectations for good behavior and godliness. When my son, Walker, became a preacher's kid, he wasn't necessarily used to being in church every Sunday or participating in all the youth group activities or being in the youth choir. Now he is at church all day on Sundays (often attending both morning worship services and then youth group that evening), and he is often asked to do behind-the-scenes jobs such as putting my music away or operating the lights for the children's choir musical.

Walker's least favorite part of being a "preacher's kid" is the fact that whenever he misbehaves, my coworkers can tell me about it at work the next day; or maybe it's the fact that sometimes I have to chaperone the trips he takes with the youth group. He has learned that there really is no hiding from his parents when he is at church, which is a good reminder that he also cannot hide from God.

"Regular" life was over when his dad married a minister, and I find myself wondering if I expect too much of my stepchildren. I certainly feel inadequate as a godly parent in my own home, but now, what if my expectation for church participation drives them away from God because they've gone from attending church in smaller doses to attending church all the time? It is a fine art, a delicate balance, and a hope that whatever I may unintentionally do to harm them, God will use for good.

Especially before marriage and parenting, my ministry career was a primary focus. It was easy to bring my work home with me—to sit on the couch in the evenings and plan an order of worship or review a new choral anthem—but now I have children who need my time, energy, and attention. Ministry consumes so much of who we are and what we do that it often becomes our life. All parents in career ministry suffer in this struggle. As stepparents, I think it is even more imperative to order our time for family. Remember that we are called to care for children who have already experienced a sense of abandonment in some form or fashion. Do they deserve to experience that hurt again because we are too busy serving God at church to serve God in our family?

I am grateful to be gainfully employed by a church that understands, encourages, and supports my children and my journey as a stepmother. My congregants often bring small gifts for the kids, give lots of hugs, and have gone out of their way to welcome two youngsters. They often affirm me as a minister to my family, telling me how I've done a great job in parenting Walker and Hope, and applaud me for taking on the challenge of making a difference in their lives. I usually squirm in my seat and think, "You have no idea how many mistakes I have made or how broken this family system is; it is only by the grace of God that we are all still alive," but I usually just say, "Thank you. It's been a long, hard journey, but we are getting through it together."

Months of counseling, prayers, and tears later, I can honestly say that we are on the way to "happily ever after," or at least toward a stepmother who isn't as wicked as she used to be. The way has been long, and the journey is certainly no yellow brick road, but our little family is learning much about how God can take what was intended for harm and turn it into something good.

Rev. Kerrie Clayton Jordan, *originally from Belhaven, North Carolina, is a graduate of East Carolina University and Campbell University Divinity School and serves First Baptist Church in Smithfield, North Carolina, as their Minister of Music and Senior Adults. Her journey as a not-so-wicked stepmother includes her husband, David; teenage son, Walker; and an imaginative daughter, Hope. Together they enjoy outdoor activities, movies, and all things musical.*

CHAPTER 10

NURTURING LIFE: A MOTHER-THEOLOGIAN REFLECTS

Nora O. Lozano

Motherhood is a blessing, a gift that I have received on two accounts. On the one hand, it is a gift that I have received throughout the years from the women who raised me. On the other hand, it is a gift that has been given to me as I have also had the privilege and joy of being a mother.

Motherhood starts in a particular moment in time, but it does not involve only that moment when a woman becomes a mother: motherhood is a lifelong journey. Once a mother, always a mother! It is a journey full of mixed feelings, emotions, and experiences, but overall I see it as a journey of nurturing other human beings in their process of becoming what God has planned for them since the beginning. It is a joyful and powerful journey because, in a sense, mothers become partners with God in this process of nurturing other human beings.

Since motherhood is a process of nurturing, I have to acknowledge that it is not circumscribed only to raising our own kids and launching them into adulthood. It may be also a process of nurturing someone else spiritually, emotionally, or intellectually. That is why many times we talk about spiritual, emotional, or intellectual mothers.

I write this reflection on motherhood as a mother and as a theologian. As I think about myself, I do not know which role carries more influence in my life. They are so intertwined. Since reflections are not done in a vacuum, I want to identify myself as a Baptist woman who looks at life and theology from a bridge. By looking from this bridge, as Leticia Guardiola-Sáenz has described it, I want to recognize and honor the experiences that identify me as a Mexican as well as a Mexican-American woman (Guardiola-Sáenz, "A Mexican-American Politics of Location: Reading from the Bridge," paper presented at the American Academy of Religion (AAR) annual meeting in Philadelphia, 1995). In some areas of the border, the Mexican and United States lands are geographically united by a bridge. This bridge helps me to imagine a cultural bridge where I can stand in order to incorporate my experiences in both cultures.

As I think about the image of this bridge, I have to recognize that this cultural bridge is not the only one that defines my life. There is also a personal bridge that incorporates my individual, most intimate life, and that connects my experiences as a mother and as a theologian. It is from these two bridges that I want to reflect today, when I am fifty-one years old and the proud biological mother of two wonderful human beings: Andrea (twenty-one years old) and Eric (fourteen years old). But also, I am the spiritual and intellectual mother/nurturer of many other children whom I cannot count anymore. And to be honest, I would never know how much I have affected their lives or how much they affected mine. I just know that under God's blessing, we encountered each other at different times, and our lives were blessed and enriched beyond what we can measure, grasp, or understand.

As I think of all these children (biological, spiritual, and intellectual), three ideas come to mind. Motherhood, this process of nurturing, is for me a journey of faith, a journey of letting go, and a journey of theological reflection.

I remember clearly the day when I found out I was expecting my first child. It was a day of joy as well as a day of surprise, as I had considered having children . . . but in the future. Since this pregnancy was a surprise, and I felt unprepared to be a mother, motherhood became a journey of faith for me from the beginning. I suspect that I am not the only one who has lived the experience of motherhood through the eyes of faith. I have noticed in both Mexico and the United States that young women who were church-goers in their early years and tend to leave during their late teens and early twenties often return to church once they become mothers. It seems that these women have a special need that makes them come back to church.

Even though there may be different explanations for this phenomenon, I came to my own conclusion once I became a mother.

I remember holding my daughter as she was a little baby and feeling for the first time a special joy that comes only with motherhood. But I also remember feeling a great sense of responsibility as I thought about the idea of taking care of her and raising her. I felt that I could not do it by myself, that I needed help from someone else. Certainly I had her dad and the older women and men in my family ready to help, but my need was beyond this kind of assistance. I needed someone superior, divine, who could guide me and encourage me. I needed someone who could reassure me that at the end things were going to be fine—not because of me or my efforts as a mother but because of divine mercy and compassion. Maybe things were not going to be exactly the way that I had pictured or planned them, but I was reassured that regardless of the outcome, God was going to be with me—with us—as a companion, guide, and protector.

This need for God's presence in my life as a mother became clearer as I started to experience what I consider one of the major defining processes of motherhood: letting go. At the beginning, my daughter and son were with me all the time, of course; they were in my womb. Then, one day they were born, and the process of separation and letting go started. I remember the first day they slept in their own rooms; it was hard. But then came the first day of leaving them in the church's nursery, the first day of day care, the first day of school, the first day of camp, the first day of college, and only God knows how many first days I will experience as a mother.

All of these first days were full of mixed emotions. On the one hand, there was a sense of celebration and accomplishment as I had the joy of observing my kids achieve a new stage in their lives. But on the other hand, these first days were also hard as they were marked by the experience of "letting go." There is much wisdom in the common saying: "letting go and letting God." Letting go of one's children and letting God take care of them is certainly a faith process. This is the only way that I have survived as a mother, believing that even though I am not around them to protect them and take care of them, God is there, all the time, protecting them and taking care of them.

But this process of letting go applies also to me as a spiritual and intellectual mother/nurturer. By the grace of God, I have been entrusted as a teacher with the minds and hearts of many pupils over the years. I have encountered these students, eager to learn, in formal academic settings and classrooms as well as in more informal settings, such as church conferences and workshops. Throughout the years, I have learned also that I need to let them go and let God continue to work on them. But learning this was not easy!

Graduations are memorable and joyful experiences. Certainly they are so for the graduates and their families and friends. They are also so for me as a professor as I see each one of my students walk proudly to the stage to receive his or her diploma. Graduations are sad too, however, as I realize that these students will not walk the halls and the classrooms of the university again on a daily basis. So I find myself with mixed feelings of celebration as well as grief. Sometimes I experience the same feeling of grief in more informal settings as I speak in conferences or workshops in different places around the world. I grieve as I think that my time with these students is over and that I may not see them again.

Throughout the years, I have learned the secret that sustains many mothers: prayer. Instead of feeling anxious regarding the place in the process where I left these students and how I could have helped them more, I recognize that I need to be grateful for our time together, let them go, and let God continue to work on them. So a prayer of gratitude for our time together, a prayer of blessing for them as they walk the next stage of the journey, and a prayer for me as I leave them in God's hands is the best response in these moments of grief.

Finally, motherhood for me has represented a rich journey of theological reflection. As a theologian, the experience of motherhood has enriched my own theological articulations and has helped me to understand God's love more clearly. When my daughter was four or five weeks old, I was in church holding her in my arms as the worship leader asked us to sing a particular hymn. I do not remember the name of the hymn, but I remember clearly its message. At a certain point it described that the love of God for humankind was such that God was willing to give up his only son as a sacrifice for the redemption of the world. As I was holding my newborn daughter, I thought, *There is no way I could do that.* I asked myself, *How is it possible that God can have that kind of love for us?* This experience helped me to understand the kind of pain God went through as he saw the suffering of his only son, as well as to capture and be grateful for God's amazing love for humanity.

Hopefully, these theological articulations are not only for my own benefit as a Christian and as a theologian. If motherhood is a process of nurturing, one way that I nurture people is through theological reflection. Theological articulation is like delivering a child. It is a process of conceiving, nurturing, and delivering a particular idea that will in the best circumstances bring liberation and abundant life to me and to the ones who have graced me with their presence as I teach, speak, or write. In this sense, I believe that I am a mother, too, as I challenge and nurture the minds and hearts of other human beings as they attempt to understand, develop, and recreate their notions of God, themselves, and the world. As we go through this process of growth and development, a new life may be conceived/imagined. I can remember particular faces at different times and places where, due to the articulation of a particular notion or idea, a new light shined, a beam of hope was born, and a new road was opened. Under God's blessing, and with the guidance of the Holy Spirit, true transformation was experienced.

As I close these reflections, I reiterate that motherhood is a gift. As all true gifts, the journey of motherhood comes with many joys and delights as well as many challenges and responsibilities. Thanks be to God that mothers have a true companion in this journey, for the giver of this gift, God, is around us helping us, protecting us, guiding us, empowering us, comforting us, smiling at us, and rejoicing with us as we, together with God, share this gift of motherhood—a journey of nurturing other human beings in their process of becoming what God has planned for them since the beginning.

———◆———

*Dr. **Nora O. Lozano** is the proud mother of Andrea and Eric. She is Associate Professor of Theological Studies at Baptist University of the Americas, and co-founder and co-director of the Latina Leadership Institute. Lozano holds an MDiv, an MPhil, and a PhD in Theological and Religious Studies. She is a member of the BWA Commission on Doctrine and Christian Unity, and attends Woodland Baptist Church in San Antonio, Texas, where she lives with her family.*

Chapter 11

Reverend Doctor Mom

Courtney Lyons

Allow me to share a few important things about myself before we get started. I am an only child, granddaughter of a preacher, and a native Texan. I thrive on challenges. During my teenage years, I had a lot of irons in the fire. I first sensed God's call to ministry just before graduating from high school at age fourteen. I was also a competitive figure skater and active in my church. In hindsight, I have no idea why I chose to major in Computer Science Engineering. I had attended Engineering Camp as a teenager—yes, I was *that* cool—and enjoyed creating designs and finding innovative solutions to problems. I was drawn to the elegance of using math: follow the rules correctly, and you will always get the right answer. No risk, just rules.

My time at the University of Texas at Arlington was wonderful. While I soaked in the college experience, I was still trying to discern how God had called me. I served on the leadership team of my Baptist Student Ministry, which continually reminded me that God had called me to something other than Computer Science Engineering. But what?

The summer before my last year of college, I heard God's voice loud and clear. After leaving a long-term abusive relationship, I felt free to follow God anywhere, and I was sure God was leading me to attend seminary to prepare for full-time ministry. At nineteen, I graduated with minors in math and psychology, served as a summer missionary in Vancouver, Canada, and then moved to Waco to attend George W. Truett Theological Seminary.

In my first semester, I took Dr. Ruth Ann Foster's Introduction to Scriptures class, and she turned my world upside down in a wonderful way. As I struggled with understanding my own call as a Baptist woman in Texas, she opened my eyes to how God had called women to ministry throughout the Bible and church history. For the first time, I finally acknowledged that God might be calling me to pastoral ministry. When Dr. Foster passed away the next year, I felt such a strong sense of responsibility to obey God's call for me, no matter what others said about God's (not) calling women. As I finished seminary, I realized that my call is to pastoral ministry through teaching higher education.

I became the youth pastor at First Baptist Marlin in 2006. I think it was there that I first became a mother. The church congregation was primarily older, entirely Caucasian, and set in an impoverished, mixed-race neighborhood that a few decades prior had been an affluent white community. There were only three youth at the church: the pianists' son, a choir member's granddaughter, and a little girl from the neighborhood named Kursten. She was eleven, smart, friendly, and hungry for love from a church family. Every week, she brought new friends, and within one year, our youth group averaged forty in attendance. While most people in the church were thrilled with our growth, a small contingent pressured the deacons to fire me for "bringing in the wrong kind of youth." I am eternally grateful to a brave interim pastor—a Truett professor, in fact—who played all his chips to defend me.

Protecting these kids' right to worship God and belong to a church family quickly made me into a Momma Bear. I called each of them weekly, helped them with their homework, attended their school functions, took them on fun outings in the church van, and helped them apply for college. I became particularly close to four of the girls. They came to rely on me so much that their mothers—all substance abusers—asked me to do a lot of "mom" things for the girls: I took them shopping for their first bras, explained how to use feminine hygiene products, and taught them how to drive.

Resigning that position was difficult, but it allowed me to focus on my studies full-time while my husband, Victor, began his first pastorate. Our new church was a family church with lots of stay-at-home mothers, and an educated, well-traveled suburbanite pastor's wife with her own sense of calling was not what they were expecting. After serving as the interim youth pastor for a short time, I resigned the position and found much more freedom to minister as a layperson. Before long, I found myself among dear friends, a loving church family.

Soon, my itch for motherhood became strong. But the realities of PhD studies required eighteen-hour days. And there is an old-school unspoken rule that women academics should not have babies until they reach tenure, normally earned around age forty. This is changing somewhat, but most women academics postpone motherhood until they are out of school, which means childrearing does not begin until the early thirties.

When I learned that I have polycystic ovarian syndrome (read: "infertility"), I decided that we needed to start trying immediately. Since most of my male colleagues already had children and faced few of the career/family dilemmas women face, I approached the graduate school about ways to better support the full well-being of all of its graduate students, male and female. The school was supportive of my suggestion for a parental leave policy for graduate students that allowed paid leave for childbirth or adoption.

Two weeks later, I was pregnant! My husband and I were overjoyed! I even preached the service in which we announced my pregnancy to the church. Pregnancy was delightful. I had no problem maintaining my coursework, and I was still skating once a week! I decorated the baby's nursery in our house and was nesting full speed ahead.

I had been invited to present a paper at the annual meeting of the biggest organization in my academic field, held the first weekend in January. I was due in mid-February and felt confident that I could present my paper in Boston and be home in plenty of time to observe the no-flying-in-the-last-month-of-pregnancy rule. My doctor cleared me for travel the day before the flight. My water broke the day after I arrived.

Labor ensued for eighteen hours with no complications, but when Stanley made his way into the world, everything changed. The doctors worked quickly and quietly, while not so subtly masking their concern. The umbilical cord was wrapped so tightly around Stanley's neck that he was not breathing. The doctors had to cut the cord immediately, even before the blood could shunt back into his body, which caused Stanley to lose around 70 percent of his blood.

I remember hanging on during those long moments of silence, crying every time I heard Stanley cry. All I could do in that moment was pray—the Romans 8:26 "groans that words cannot express" kind of praying. The medical team let me see Stanley before taking him to the NICU. As I spoke his name, he opened his eyes and locked them on me. I will never forget that feeling of connection with my son.

Because of some complications, I could not see Stanley again for seven hours, but I was informed that an emergency blood transfusion had saved his life. The nurse brought me a picture of Stanley, and I could not believe how strong he looked already. When I held him for the first time, I was overwhelmed by how tiny and perfect he was and how God had protected us.

I am convinced that my boy was born in Boston, at Massachusetts General Hospital—the best neonatal hospital in the world—by design, and that's coming from an Arminian! After eight days in the NICU, we flew home to Texas. When we walked into our house, we found that our church family had filled our living room with baby gear and our refrigerator with food. Overwhelming love.

I stayed home for two Sundays after we returned home. As tired as I was, I eased back into church attendance by teaching my Sunday school class and staying in the service until Stanley woke from his nap, at which time I would step out with him until church dismissed. Because there was no nursery, Stanley came to Sunday school with me. If he awoke, class members enjoyed feeding him and holding him. I worried that I had disrespected the class by bringing a crying baby, but seeing me as a frazzled, vulnerable parent helped class members connect with me and facilitated a tremendous amount of respect and trust within our group.

Victor was sure that God was calling him to church-plant. Beginning a new ministry is a lot like caring for a newborn baby—and it meant a 20 percent decrease in our household income. A few months into the new work, Victor decided to return to seminary for a Doctor of Ministry. I was still a full-time PhD student, in my last semester of coursework, and preparing for comprehensive exams. Oh, and did I mention I was nursing, too?

As natural as it seems, nursing requires practice, dedication, and enormous amounts of time and often comes with social difficulties. At church, I received criticism for "indecency" for nursing in an office with the door closed under a nursing cover. I was also criticized for not nursing when I gave Stanley a bottle (even a bottle of pumped breast milk!). Needing to pump or nurse often, I searched for an appropriate place on campus—not a bathroom—but found nothing. In response to my expressed concerns, Baylor opened its first nursing room on campus, available to students, faculty, and staff.

By the end of one semester, Victor and I realized we needed full-time childcare, which was a difficult decision. Friends and family rearranged schedules and worked hard to help us, but we needed a more permanent solution. We were surprised by how much Stanley thrives in day care! After "school," Stanley and I enjoy the evening as special family time.

One of the most difficult aspects of motherhood and ministry for me is that women in ministry are in a fishbowl *under a spotlight* since we press the traditional limits of femininity. Mother-ministers are in an exceptionally scrutinized fishbowl because we are judged by how well we perform all of our functions as minister, wife, *and* mother. Congregants demanded the same level of pastoral care from me as I gave them before Stanley was born, even while many criticized my decisions to remain in school, place Stanley in childcare, and continue skating weekly. I choose to believe that they meant well, but I felt pressure compounding from every direction. I was under significant psychological distress for several months.

Shortly after Stanley was born, I learned that Kursten, from my FBC Marlin youth group, was four months pregnant at age fifteen. She had little help or guidance. In true Momma Bear fashion, I made sure she received medical care, helped provide maternity clothes, and informed her of adoption and parenting options. Kursten feared God would take back her call to ministry since she had "messed up." In those vulnerable moments, we talked through the beauty of God's redemption and desire to use anyone with a surrendered heart.

As I was wrestling with the decision to wean Stanley, I got the call that Kursten was in labor. If I went one more day pumping instead of nursing, I was going to lose my supply. As I drove to the hospital, my heart was filled with mixed emotions, but I knew Kursten needed me.

When I arrived, I found all of my Marlin girls around her bedside. After Kursten delivered baby Austin, her parents went home; they did not even wait for her to be moved to a recovery room before they left. This sweet, scared sixteen-year-old mother was alone in a huge delivery room with her new son, and I knew why God wanted me there. I stayed and taught her how to nurse and how to be a mother, even as I was just learning myself. That night was one of the most formative experiences in my motherhood-ministry life. I caught a glimpse of the depth and beauty of Christ's incarnation and of how much womanhood resembles the image of God.

I grieved the end of my nursing days with Stanley, sobbing inconsolably. The silver lining was that my relationship with Stanley was no longer filled with anxiety about milk supply. I could now just relax in his presence. In the long run, I think he benefited more from me being relaxed around him than from breast milk.

After I passed comprehensive exams, I felt able to invest more in the new church plant. I sang with the worship team (while holding Stanley through rehearsal and sometimes the service!), coordinated the educational ministries of the church, taught Wednesday night Bible study, and mentored the youth minister. But as a parent, I now faced the dilemma of trying to do all of these things while watching a baby. Since Stanley was the only baby in the church, we didn't have a nursery system. Thankfully, our mother church offered to fund a nursery worker.

I struggle with how to handle those scenarios. Do I patiently accept that motherhood sometimes trumps ministry? Do I speak against the double standard that even though Stanley's father and I are both ministers in our church, the prevailing assumption is that the mother alone is responsible for Stanley's care? I love my son and treasure the opportunity to care for him, but I grieve the unfair situations women in ministry face.

For me, the key to juggling motherhood, ministry, and scholarship is self-care. I spend Saturday mornings doing something I love: figure skating, a physical, creative outlet that is like psychological detox for me. I think every minister needs something they can do regularly for spiritual and psychological renewal. I am a better minister and mother because of taking this time for self-care.

I also meet monthly with a covenant group of women in ministry in my area. Four of the five of us are mothers. I am so thankful to have a safe place to share—honestly and fully—my burdens in ministry and family. I know they will respond with compassion, encouragement, and accountability. Being a woman in ministry can be lonely, but just as we live in families and worship in churches—even as God is relational as Trinity—we are meant to be in relationship with each other.

Stanley is two now, learning new things, taking on new challenges, and growing in so many ways. Though I feel the pull of school and church responsibilities, I will always put Stanley first. I work diligently during the daytime so that our evenings are *ours*. I hope that being a model of a healthy balance between work and family will be an encouragement to Stanley that he can pursue his dreams *and* be a wonderful parent at the same time.

I look forward to beginning the teaching ministry I have been preparing for since 1999. I am not sure what lies ahead. The mathematician in me doesn't like when variables outnumber constants. But ministry-motherhood has helped me to treasure this constant: the God who calls also equips, protects, and sustains those who follow the call.

Being a mother has opened my eyes to how God wants to relate to humanity. God's womb surrounds, nurtures, and forms us. God's milk nourishes us perfectly. God sings us lullabies and rocks us to sleep. God invites us to play in ways that strengthen our bodies for taking our first steps. God knows where we dropped our sippy cups and kisses our ouchies. God likes to make us laugh by creating silly faces on our pancakes and hiding sweet notes in our lunch boxes. As I love my son through all of his ups and downs, I am continually awed at God's faithful love for me through all of mine. I am beckoned into the presence of Christ, invited to treasure these divine moments in my heart as Mary did for her son, and strengthened to continue preaching the good news. I am a better mother because I am a minister. I am a better minister because I am a mother. In all things, God is faithful.

———•◆•———

*Rev. **Courtney Lyons** is Stanley's mom. She is a PhD candidate at Baylor University, studying American religion and social justice. She teaches Introduction to Christian Scriptures and Christian Heritage at Baylor, where she also helped create a graduate student parental leave policy and a nursing room on campus. Courtney has trained in figure skating since 1992 and is now a coach. She was ordained at Seventh and James Baptist Church in Waco, Texas (CBF) in 2008.*

CHAPTER 12

THE CRAZY BEAUTIFUL: RAISING OUR FAMILY IN THE INNER CITY

Angel Pittman

It was really just a typical street in inner-city Detroit. Looking left, the roll call of homes from one corner to the next read half boarded-up house selling drugs; vacant lot terribly overgrown; uninhabited house with boarded-up windows; occupied old house with peeling paint, sofas, and chairs scattered around the large porch.

"So what do you think of this house?" my husband asked as I tore myself away to look at the house on the other side of the street. "Are you crazy?" I responded. "You can't be serious!" As I rattled off my list of reasons for *never* wanting to live on this street, I include the words "crack house." Having lived in a poor neighborhood previously, I recognized the signs of drug dealing just from our few minutes sitting in our car on the street, as folks walked or rolled up on bikes in a steady stream for unusually quick visits to the house. Disappointed that I had rejected yet another of his offerings without even seeing the inside, my husband started the car and on we rolled through the streets of Detroit, searching for what would become our new home.

I was struggling. I knew that the Lord had placed a calling in our hearts not only to share our lives with the poor and hurting but also to go deeper. We felt called to model the kind of relocation seen in Jesus' example recorded in John 1:14, "And the Word became flesh and blood and moved into the neighborhood" (*The Message*). So that's what we had done since the beginning of our marriage, as a young couple fresh out of college serving in a local faith-based nonprofit ministry in central Texas. We lived in the community that we served.

Jason and I married just seven days after graduation and began working side by side in nonprofit ministry. We purchased our first home in a low-income neighborhood in Texas just six months after graduation—not so hard to do on our meager salary when our 4,000-square foot fixer-upper cost the same as most people's first car. With the help of our homeless friends who moved us in, our crazy life of living in the inner city began.

During our years in Texas, we had lived and worked in our community long enough that we didn't race to the window every time we heard gunshots. We knew how to shut down a drug house, we knew a thing or two about scams—having been the victim a few times too many—and we learned the difference a listening ear can make. We walked people out of addiction into freedom, we counseled, we prayed, and we saw lives change, but we certainly didn't claim to know it all.

"Yeah, Roderick just mowed our lawn. Why do you ask?" I asked our neighbor who'd called. "Well, he's walking past my house with your mower now," she replied. I was figuring out a bit too late that the boy who asked to mow our lawn for $20 thought the deal came with the mower. During our Texas years, we began to refer to the items stolen from our home after having guests over, folks that most people might not even open the front door to, simply as "parting gifts." It was indeed a crazy life, but it was beautiful, too.

In spring 1999 after four years of ministry and marriage, we were joyfully awaiting the birth of our first son, Isaac. Before the baby was even a bump, our parents and other "more responsible adults" started asking where we were going to move now that we had a baby on the way. It may have seemed strange to others that we routinely let all sorts of people live in our home: a teenage expectant mother, college kids, or young adults wanting to try out this crazy inner-city life. Our house was nearly always full. Sure, we welcomed homeless folks in regularly for our Bible studies and visits, and yes, we spent Christmas Day with a pretty eclectic crew of folks who needed a place to belong. It certainly didn't look like the life of most of our friends as they settled into suburban America. But we loved it, and we weren't going to move just because our family was expanding.

We were learning to live our lives with open hands—our possessions could walk away at any time and did with some frequency—and open hearts, because you just never knew where a good friend might come from or look like. Take Johnny, one our close friends for many years. For most young college students, having a homeless man on a bike catch you off guard at night as you are exiting your car might be frightening and convince them to be much more wary. But instead, that encounter began a long friendship for Johnny and me that continued through the birth of our son, Isaac, six years later. Johnny was excited there was a baby on the way, too, and he would regularly bring us specially baby-selected items that he found from his daily perusals of the dumpsters. Many a toy was scrubbed and sanitized to become Isaac's favorites. Crazy? Yes, but beautiful. Our acceptance of Johnny's friendship and his gifts allowed him to be a part of my son's life for many years.

I loved that just touching my baby boy could bring tears to the eyes of men toughened from years on the streets. Men who usually saw mothers pull their children closer as they crossed paths stroked our son's sweet head or clutched his tiny fist. They opened their hearts to share untold stories of how circumstances and mistakes led to broken families and children they hadn't seen for decades.

Our first son, Isaac, was dedicated to the Lord amid homeless folks and former drug addicts as he turned a year old. During a beautiful ceremony at our church, Church Under the Bridge, our pastor likened our calling to that of Abraham offering up his son Isaac in obedience to the Lord at the altar. In many of the same ways, we've seen protection for our son and our family as we have chosen to continue our calling of living and working in the inner city.

After several years, Jason felt the urge to increase his learning, earning two Master's degrees in social work and divinity. Many believed we had finally come to our senses, and now, with more degrees, we were finally going to end our work in the inner city and help people less dirty, less scary, and less urban. Much to their surprise, we took our learning and our then-seven years' experience and moved into inner-city Detroit—a whole new level of urban living in a bigger city with more gangs and more violence.

We didn't need to share statistics about Detroit with curious friends. Everyone knew it was a tough place, and secretly I was having a hard time trusting the Lord with this next step. Needing time, we extended a month-to-month lease in the suburban ring just outside Detroit. I spent some real time pleading with God to give me the strength to take the plunge into this new and unknown urban chaos, even as we continued to house hunt now with the surprise of a second baby on the way.

And so here we were spending hours and hours driving through Detroit trying to find a home near the target neighborhood we felt led to serve alongside. We'd been to several homes advertised as "Ready to move in" only to find them boarded up and covered with graffiti. We finally found a home on a quiet and unusually secluded street—so secluded, in fact, that it was closed to all traffic, a major deterrent to drive-by shootings if you can't drive down the street, apparently. The house was old and beautiful from the pictures, but when we finally toured it my heart sank. It wasn't right. Not only was it smaller than expected but we also knew we couldn't practice our usual ministry of hospitality in a home where folks would have to walk two blocks just to get to our front door. The disappointment and exhaustion from months of searching was evident on our faces. Noticing this, the home-owner said, "Well, I do have another home. It's on an open street and is much larger, but the neighborhood isn't as nice." "Let's see it!" we nearly screamed as we headed to our cars.

It was now dark as we followed her to the house, parking directly out front on the dimly lit street. We walked to the door. Inside it was perfect: big and open with more than enough bedrooms for our growing family and the interns we were expecting soon. We were ready to sign the lease right then. As the owner prepared the documents, my husband pulled me aside, saying, "I need to show you something."

Jason guided me back to the front door, and, holding it open, he asked me to step onto the porch. "Do you recognize this street?" My eyes scanned the homes across the street from left to right and there they were: abandoned house, vacant lot, abandoned and uninhabited house, large old house. "Is this really it? Are you sure? Did you know?" The questions tumbled out of my mouth. Never great directionally, I hadn't recognized the house in the dark. But Jason knew this house and this street very well. He'd looked at the house from the outside several times as it was just a few blocks from the ministry we had begun working with and even closer to the church we'd begun attending, but he had never wanted to push me to go back to it and look at the inside. Jason had been waiting nearly four months for the Lord to work on my heart and bring me back to this home. It was in this home, surrounded by bulletproof glass at every business in our neighborhood, that we welcomed our second son, Lucas.

We lived on that typical Detroit street in our big, old house for several years with not a single incident. This was despite grave warnings from the two Detroit officers—not exactly the best welcoming committee—who responded when we accidentally tripped the house alarm while moving in. The officers berated us for daring to move into the African-American community and told us, as they stomped off our porch, that when things got bad, "Don't call us! We warned you!" Things never got bad. Sure, there were crazy moments, like when a drug dealer tried to pay me off after I accidentally backed into his car on our street. But we were getting more and more used to accepting such crazy moments as part of our usual routines.

Our years in Detroit were full of learning and new experiences not only for us but also for our son Isaac. Upon moving to the big city at age three, Isaac was beginning to notice the subtleties of urban life more and more. One day after he saw me give cash to a neighbor at the door, and then later saw me give a homeless man at McDonald's a coupon for a free sandwich, he said, "Oh, I get it, Mom! We give money to people we know and coupons to people we don't know." My young son was outlining the untold principle Jason and I had developed over the years. While taking care to acknowledge and affirm the dignity of all those asking from us, we learned from years of working with the chronically homeless and addicted that a cash handout is never *really* helpful.

Isaac's learning continued. The truth of unequal schools came through neighbor kids complaining about having to bring toilet paper to school and not having art or PE classes. Isaac found out about the differences in city services when it took far longer to conquer riding a bike with no training wheels on sidewalks torn up from old trees in a city that didn't make even minor street repairs. He learned about race later than most, as he had to be told he was actually white and his friends were black, having never heard Jason or me refer to someone by the color of their skin. He was thoroughly confused by Black History Month in school. "But Mommy, my friends are brown and I'm peach!" A much more adequate picture of the skin tones around us, we agreed.

On the weekend of his first birthday, Lucas, like his older brother, was dedicated to the Lord at our church. We vowed with our Detroit congregation, to help Lucas grow to be a healer in hurting communities just like his biblical namesake, Luke. Our pastor emphasized that part of my and Jason's ministry was to be an example to our son of bringing healing and justice to those who were hurting.

Since 2005, we've lived and ministered in inner-city Miami, in the historic African-American neighborhood Overtown. My husband and I now direct a nonprofit, Touching Miami with Love. Ours is the neighborhood most people avoid when they can and lock their doors, looking straight ahead, if they mistakenly drive through. Gunshots are common background noise, rap music blares until the wee hours of the morning, the lights blink yellow so no one stops and risks getting carjacked. The traffic from the highways overhead that destroyed our community creates a constant buzz. The scream of sirens and the whirl of helicopters closing in as they shine spotlights on the streets below are part of the ambiance. We're used to finding alternate routes home because of streets closed due to police activity. On a regular basis, teddy bears cluster in makeshift memorials for the latest victims of violence. Prostitutes walk up and down the block, sometimes so strung out that we wonder if they know where they are. We spent months keeping our second-floor bedroom windows closed to prevent our boys from watching as drug addicts shot up below, and we waited for our calls to the city to be answered. Police tase and arrest folks across the street while I chat with neighbors on the sidewalk and our kids zoom by us on bikes. Teens not too much older than my own son make drug deals in front of the corner store down the street.

It's often crazy, and folks question the wisdom of choosing to raise our family here. But because we have the privilege of working in a ministry where lives are being transformed and cycles of poverty are being broken, my children are also learning hands-on compassion. And it's beautiful. Other families in gated communities, spacious homes with large manicured lawns, and ethno-centric neighborhoods have to pay thousands of dollars to send their kids on mission trips to neighborhoods like mine so they can learn compassion. I know this well because part of my work is facilitating those groups all year long.

My kids get to join us in our ministry, playing alongside the kids in summer camp or volunteering for special projects. I don't have to take my boys anywhere else to teach them compassion, understanding, grace, the value of living simply, and how to be grateful for what they have. We get to show love at the park across the street where tons of kids play unsupervised until far after dark. We stop by our library packed with youth and adults waiting to get on the computers and feel righteous anger at the inequities of technology. We have a neighbor boy over to play who, though years older than my younger son, can't read the instructions to the board game, and we get to show understanding and empathy. We stop and wait patiently for the mentally ill woman wandering aimlessly in the street to allow our car to pass and get to practice grace. We walk to the corner and see the man whose feet were amputated from unchecked diabetes and share compassion. We ride the metro with the homeless man we know by name who talks to an unseen someone the whole time, and we model kindness.

My children get to live and breathe opportunities for compassion because they see need at their door. They ask questions.

"Where's that kid's mom?"

"Why are so many people in line at the library?"

"Why can't Travis read if he's in fourth grade?"

"Why is that lady standing in the street, Mom?"

"What happened to that man's feet?"

"Isn't that Roger, Mom?"

They ask questions *every* day because they are kids. And because I'm their mom, I get to answer them . . . with the big, ugly truth of the consequences of poverty, parents too young and uneducated with no good examples to parent their kids positively, how the unemployment gap is deepening in our neighborhood as more and more job applications are only offered online, the failings of our schools and a messed up educational system, drugs and the spiral toward homelessness, the injustice of health care, the sad truth of how America treats our mentally ill veterans.

And they don't just listen and nod—no way. They plan and they invite and they befriend and they reach out in natural, easy ways that show immense compassion, with ideas and plans that embarrass me as the adult for not having thought of them first. And so, for nearly twenty years of living in the inner city, over thirteen of those years as a mom, I can say, "Yes, raising your kids in the inner city *is* crazy, but it's beautiful!"

------ ◆ ------

*A graduate of Baylor University, **Angel Pittman** serves as Assistant Director alongside her college sweetheart husband, Jason, at Touching Miami with Love, an urban ministry in the historic African-American neighborhood of Overtown. Angel's education background shaped after-school programs in Texas, Detroit, and at TML as Children's Director, creating the ToMorrow's Leaders Program. She is also field personnel with the Cooperative Baptist Fellowship. Her passions are reading and writing about racial reconciliation, government policies and the poor, suburban and urban realities, and raising children in the inner city. The Pittmans have two sons, Isaac and Lucas.*

CHAPTER 13

A LIMP, A BLESSING, AND A NEW NAME

Alicia Davis Porterfield

Everyone told me I would be different once I became a mother. I knew they were right, in the same way I knew that labor would be hard (as people kept telling me, "there's a reason they call it 'labor'"). I was like a toddler hearing that touching a hot stove will burn you. I knew the truth in theory only: a cerebral knowledge, not a deep-down, cell-level knowledge.

I had wanted to be a mother for over a year before I became pregnant. Many others struggle much longer and choose different roads, but even just a few months of trying was plenty of time for me to begin questioning God. In good Old Testament fashion, I started asking "How long, O Lord?" before it had been long at all. I found a new sisterhood with Sarah, Rachel, and Hannah, all of whom struggled with what the King James Version calls being "barren." My heart began to feel barren, but I took solace from their stories, much starker than mine. I so wanted to help bring a new life into the world.

As the first year rolled around, we took a small first step toward a medical intervention and waited. Finally, a plus sign appeared on the magic little stick! New life was coming! Actually, new life was coming sooner than we thought. The pregnancy was farther along than anyone knew: twelve weeks instead of seven or eight.

But the way we found out was filled with deep fear and grief. I began bleeding and cramping one Saturday night, and after hearing a description of my symptoms, our doctor diagnosed a miscarriage over the phone. Our bed was wet with tears that night, and there I stayed all the next day, as my husband, Eric, went to lead Sunday services at our church. Huddled in our bed, I read the stories of pioneer women, spiritual offspring of our biblical mothers. I found comfort and connection as I read their stories of enduring wagon trains and deep pain and loss, all to make a new life in a new land.

But—a gospel word if there ever was one—things were not what they seemed. A trip to the doctor to confirm a miscarriage and prepare for next steps transformed our grief when a little heartbeat made itself known, still thrumming and growing. The doctor said the symptoms of miscarriage may have just been a belated menstrual cycle; apparently, they do not always end with pregnancy, as I had been told for years. But it was the last one I had that pregnancy, and I never had one during the two pregnancies that followed. As a healthcare chaplain, I knew that medicine is a "practice" and rarely has all the answers we want. Put plainly, no one really knew what had happened. But our baby was alive. New life was coming.

So grateful, I welcomed the common challenges of pregnancy: first-trimester nausea and sleepiness, a burgeoning waist, going on the gestational diabetes-prevention diet (though I missed my milkshakes terribly), tiredness, fluctuating hormones, fluctuating internal temperature (I almost froze my husband that summer as we awaited a September due date). Like many expectant mothers, I dreamed about our baby and thought about how everything I did could affect him. Then something happened that I had no control over: his amniotic fluid was low, and the doctor prescribed bed rest for the last six weeks.

Ah, bed rest. It sounds so wonderful, so inviting after all the work of pregnancy, baby preparations, ministry work, and everyday demands. And for the first few days it was nice, peaceful and quiet. Then I got lonely . . . and bored . . . and listless. I read all four Harry Potter novels in print at the time, the Lord of the Rings series, and as many mysteries as friends and church members could share. I worked on thank-you notes. I prayed. I wrote. I waited. It was work. *But not nearly as bad as what many go through*, I kept reminding myself.

And then came the thirty-seven-and-a-half-week mark when the doctor was ready to induce labor. Induction: a "science"-sounding word for an unnatural process. As I would find out with our third child, non-induced labor is intense enough. Medicinally induced labor forces the body into labor early, making everything particularly intense. Again, this was one of the things I heard and understood cognitively but could not possibly truly understand—yet. About eight hours later, I got it: mind, body, and soul.

After one particularly hard moment in labor, my mind floated away from the present and wondered limply, but desperately, if maybe we could all just go home and try again tomorrow. No such luck. Another contraction jerked me into the present before I could think anything else. My birth plan, so ignorantly and studiously written weeks before, had declared that I would ask for pain-relief measures when I needed them. I needed them about an hour before I asked for them, and then said relief took a while to get to the room and then into my system. I thanked God that I was not a pioneer woman.

The baby's head was huge: "He's got the head of a nine pounder!" our labor and delivery nurse exclaimed. Everybody laughed—except me. After an hour of pushing, weeks of bed rest, and an episiotomy to avoid worse tearing, I was exhausted. Out came the suction device to help him (and me) out. I thanked God I wasn't born in biblical times.

Finally, body ripped and cut, legs trembling from the pushing process, every muscle limp, I saw him come into the world and heard his cry. Covered in blood and white stuff (called vernix, it protects the baby's skin in the uterus, but I couldn't call up that fun fact at the moment), he was beautiful and messy, as was the whole process. The nurse placed him on my tummy, and he and I looked at each other, blinking in wonder and a little bit of fear. Then he was whisked away for tests and cleaning and I was jerked out of wonder into more pushing (to get the placenta out), with the nurse kneading my stomach with her fist like a sadistic masseuse. And then came the fun of being sewn back together.

My heart felt as torn as my body as I waited for our baby to be returned to me. Already, I longed for him, couldn't wait to hold him near again, skin to skin. We'd been so close for nine months; even as exhausted as I was, my arms felt strangely empty without him now that he was in the world with me. Numb with the shock of all I'd experienced the last ten hours, I felt cracked and painfully vulnerable.

I wanted my son's birth to be amazingly powerful and profound. It was—just not in the ways I had imagined. It was . . . *traumatic.* Knowing that others had gone through much worse, I fished around for a different word, but that one kept coming to the surface in the days after he was born. Weeks later, I read the definition: "a deeply distressing or disturbing experience." I thought, "Yep. That's it." But I couldn't say it out loud. No one seemed to want to hear it, and I felt guilty about feeling so tired and shaken—so traumatized—by the experience. I felt somehow "un-motherly" because I found labor and delivery to be so *awful,* as well as awe-full.

But in the months to come, I wrestled with what had happened to me. Always a theological processor, I needed to make sense of what had happened to us, our new baby and me. I was profoundly changed: marked by carrying him for nine months, sharing body systems with him, feeding him with every bite I took, feeling him turn and kick within me—but even more so by giving birth to him. And my heart would never be the same, either. My mind churned around this new little reality in our lives; my heart newly reshaped around him.

This gave me a deep, profound gratefulness to all the mothers in the world, including my own. Now I knew what people meant when they said that becoming a mother would change me—or at least, I was working out what that change had wrought in me. While our newborn slept, I read the newspaper, trying to catch up on what was happening in the world. When I came across photos of mothers and babies in war-scarred areas, children malnourished by famine and poverty, or accounts of abuse or neglect, my stomach literally hurt. I felt as if my body now understood why the words *womb* and *mercy* share the same root in Hebrew (Jer 31:20). The suffering of children and mothers around the world suddenly settled much closer to my heart and deeper in my bones. I prayed for God's mercy for them with a guttural fervor I hadn't known.

As my body healed and the baby and I found our rhythm for nursing, I still pondered the changes in me. I'd lost that just-after-birth feeling that my insides were sliding around and bound to lose their place. But my balance was still off sometimes, as if my hips were not back to home base and might never be. The stretch marks that decorated the bottom of my fully pregnant belly now made their visual debut as I deflated. Looking in the mirror after a hard-won shower was now to be strictly avoided. I looked like I'd been through something very hard. I had. But I couldn't say so.

Still, I could mull over Scripture while I nursed the baby or walked him around during late-night crying bouts, changed diaper after diaper and gingerly bathed this tiny, slippery creature. I needed to be grounded in the Story that had shaped my life; it seemed like the only thing holding me together. Two images kept coming to me: Jacob, now Israel, walking away with a limp and a blessing from his wrestling match with the Holy, and Mary, poor obscure girl turned pregnant prophet (Gen 32:22-32; Luke 1:26-56).

Jacob and his muddy wrestling match with God (or an angel or a man; scholars differ) by the river Jabbok felt just about right for what labor had been like for me. At the Jabbok, Jacob was facing his past and his future, his wrongs and his pending reunion with Esau. I wasn't facing any wrongs, per se, but labor was a reckoning of sorts, a river to cross. Once labor began in earnest, there was no stopping it. Once the Holy got hold of Jacob, there was no stopping it. Labor felt like a wrestling match, dirty and messy, so intimate in its closeness, full of grunts and groans, bodies that feel out of control, contorted in the moment. But God would not let go, holding Jacob close, honoring the striving of this human, full of weakness and foolishness, beloved.

To end the match before dawn, God strikes Jacob on the hip socket, giving him a limp, a permanent souvenir from his ordeal. But before he will let go of the Holy, Jacob demands a blessing and gets it, along with a new name. He becomes "Israel, for you have striven with God and with humans and have prevailed" (Gen 32:28; NRSV). I got my blessing, too: this baby, this new me. I got my limp: a changed body, heart, and mind, a permanent souvenir. And I got a new name: Mama. It was a messy, intimate, grunt-worthy ordeal, but it had to happen before we could cross the river together.

Mary would also become Mama, but not before she became Prophet Mary, telling the good news of her coming child and Savior to Elizabeth, her kinswoman (Luke 1:46-56). Mary took the angel at his word and, calling on the prophets of old, told what God had done in calling her to bear the Messiah. Already, even before the child drew breath, Mary named the reversals God brings and the fulfillment God offers: "He has brought down the powerful from their thrones, and has lifted up the lowly; he has filled the hungry with good things, and sent the rich away empty" (1:52-53). Mary boldly told the story God gave her, claiming the truth for herself and all the world, regardless of what others may think.

Earlier, I had seen a Christmas card where the artist painted the earth within Mary's pregnant belly. The image stuck with me, recalling the Greek Orthodox Church's name for Mary, *Theotokos*, meaning "God bearer." In bearing God the Son to us, Mary gave us hope for the world. She bore the Story to us and for us. And she was brave enough to claim that Story, as a prophet, then a mother, and then a disciple.

It has taken me years to claim my traumatic wrestling match of a birth story, to become like Mary and tell what God has done with, through, in, and for me. I am still pondering it, in fact, as motherhood transitions into different seasons. My oldest child is now eleven as I write this. He has two younger brothers with their own birth stories, each of which are precious and changed me, too. But the first one, quite literally, plowed the way.

Being a child-bearer changed me in body, mind, and soul. Bringing new life into the world cost something. I bear the scars and the limp and also bear the blessings and the story. I am changed, as surely as I am changed through God's redeeming, saving, sacrificing love. Now I have the tiniest taste of what bringing new life costs. And I am so humbled, so grateful, so blessed.

------- ◆ -------

An Atlanta native, **Rev. Alicia Davis Porterfield** *earned a BSEd from the University of Georgia and an MDiv and ThM from Duke University Divinity School. A Board Certified Chaplain, she completed two residencies and served as chaplain for a retirement village in Pinehurst, North Carolina. Alicia and her husband, Eric, also a pastor, are grateful to be learning, growing, reading, and singing with Davis (11), Luke (9), and Thomas (7).*

CHAPTER 14

A JOURNEY TO FAMILY

Susie C. Reeder

I had always dreamed I would be a mother. From the time I was a little girl, I knew what I would name my children: a little girl named Amy Elizabeth and a boy named Mark Anthony. But as I was about to turn forty and serving as a full-time ordained minister in a church, that dream had not come true. Because I was not married, I worked many hours in my church. I loved my youth and found joy in taking others' children to movies and going out to eat.

But in 1999, I took thirteen teenagers and three other adults to Nairobi, Kenya, on a mission trip. In preparation, I had been praying that God would change lives on that trip, never realizing that He was about to change mine. Because of my role as minister to youth, we visited an orphanage in the Dandora Slum of Nairobi, Kenya, in order to learn about the children's lives. While I was there, I remember thinking that even though it would be best for a two-parent family to adopt a child, having one parent was better than no parent.

Two years later, I sat having a conversation with a good friend over dinner and voiced aloud for the first time that I wanted to adopt. "Why don't you?" my friend asked. I responded that I'm single, I work in a church, and I don't have any money. He looked at me and said, "If it's something God wants you to do, He'll provide a way. " I knew I believed that, but trusting God to provide was a little harder. So my journey began.

Our Youth Ministry Council chooses a theme each summer for our youth ministry's Bible study. The theme we chose that summer was from a Kyle Matthews song titled "See for Yourself." Some of the lyrics are,

See for yourself, God is alive, workin' the world, concerned with your life.
He's where he said he would be, with the last and the least,
So you don't have to take it from me,
When you help someone else you can see for yourself.

As we met for our first summer Bible study in 2001, I committed to "see for myself" what God was going to do in my own life. I began to pray for God to show me the way.

The next week I took my youth to a camp called Passport. Each summer Passport Youth Camps identifies a mission cause for the participants to support financially. When we arrived at Passport, we found that the mission offering was going to an adoption agency called Dillon International. Dillon was raising funds for humanitarian work at an orphanage in South Vietnam. That week we heard the story of little Anna: she told of her birth mother caring enough to give her up for adoption and how her new family loved her. Later in the week we watched a video of children orphaned in Vietnam. My heart hurt knowing that I could love and provide a home for a child who did not have a family. At the end of the week, one of my youth asked me if I thought those videos were a sign from God. I did!

The first of July, we left on our youth mission trip to Hobart, Oklahoma. My job was to motivate the teenagers to accomplish their goals during the week. Little did I know that I would meet a little girl named Hannah who would affect my life.

Each afternoon we held a day camp for children, ages four years to sixth grade. A two-year-old girl named Hannah showed up with her two older sisters. A woman brought them each day, and I thought the woman was their mother. I found out later the woman was their aunt; their mother was in prison. I ended up playing with Hannah throughout the week, and my heart grew for her. By the end of our trip, Hannah would not leave my arms.

On the last day, we went to a lake for some recreation. Hannah's family came with us. I played with Hannah in the sand. When it was time to leave, I took Hannah back to her aunt and grandmother, and she began to cry. As I turned to walk away, Hannah cried harder and yelled, "Mommy, Mommy!" At that moment, I knew in my heart that there was a child somewhere who didn't have a mom or dad to care for them, but I could. God was helping me to "see for myself." I was ready for the next step of the journey.

Not everyone was so supportive. Many wondered how I would continue my role as youth minister and also be a single mom. My pastor even told me that I should go to the personnel committee for approval. I remember thinking that was absurd. If I had been married and gotten pregnant, would I have to go to the personnel committee for approval? Ultimately, I knew that God had called me to ministry, *and* God was calling me to adopt.

By the end of the summer, I was ready to move forward. I had talked with many families who had adopted and was ready to choose a local agency. I had written for information from Dillon International and became a frustrated when I didn't hear anything from them. Eventually, I decided to go with the local agency instead. But on the very day I planned to mail in my application, three different people said to me, "Did you consider Dillon International?" Taking this as another sign, I finally called them and found they had sent my packet to the right city but the wrong state. In the end, I did choose Dillon International and felt that God was leading me to adopt from China, where little girls were abandoned just because they were female.

At this point in the process, I read a book titled *Let Prayer Change Your Life* by Becky Tirabassi (Nashville: Oliver Nelson, 2000). Becky, who also was a youth minister, says, "My appointments with God often contained conversations that turned into hopes, then became goals that structured plans and ultimately turned into accomplishments." Becky's book led me to begin journaling my prayers. It was amazing how God began to answer them. My hopes were turning into plans. My adoption process led me on a prayer journey.

By October 2001, I had mailed the formal application to adopt from China. On November 13, my case manager from Dillon called to tell me that things had changed for single parents adopting from China. A quota system had been put in place, and not as many singles would get to adopt. I probably would not get one of the spots. I was so disappointed.

God gave me Romans 12 to read that night. I wrote in my prayer journal, "It says in verse two, 'let God transform you into a new person by changing the way you think—then you will know what God wants you to do.' God, that is my prayer." Later in verse 12, it says, "Be glad for all God is planning for you. Be patient in trouble and always be prayerful." So I prayed over all my choices again: Ukraine, Guatemala, India, and a new program opening up in Vietnam.

On November 15, I decided to adopt from Vietnam. Never would I have imagined that God would have me to go to Vietnam to find my daughter. But as I looked back, it was all part of God's plan. Vietnam wasn't even a choice when I started out, and it only became available when China closed for me. This all brought me full circle to where I started: watching a video of orphaned children in Vietnam at Passport Youth Camp. God was preparing the way, and I would be the first to adopt from Vietnam with Dillon International.

Then came more paperwork, fingerprints, and a home study. The home study included the first big amount of money due in the process. I needed $1,200 and had only $120. At our staff Christmas party, I opened my envelope that usually contained a $25-50 Christmas gift from our church. This time I opened it and found $1,200, just the amount needed. Our church staff had all donated their gifts because they wanted to be in on the beginning stages of helping bring my little girl home. I was ready for the next step of the journey.

On Monday, March 18, 2002, I slept in after working most of Saturday and Sunday. I knew a referral was close but was quite surprised when my case manager called and said, "Susie, I have your referral." I had to get out of bed to write down the information. Nguyen Thi Ha was her name, and she went by Ha. She was the oldest little girl in the orphanage in Vinh Long, Vietnam. Yes, that *was* the orphanage to which my youth had given their mission offering the summer before at Passport Camp! I couldn't get the computer on fast enough to see her picture. I called my sister while I was pulling up the picture, and we were both screaming. Her name would be Hannah Ha, named after the little girl I met in Oklahoma.

I'm not going to say it was an easy journey. Adoption is never easy. At one point, we didn't know if the adoption would happen, as the Vietnamese government began closing adoptions with the United States. Then I had to travel to Vietnam with a three-day notice. There were *two* trips to Vietnam, which meant more money and being separated for three months after meeting my little Hannah on the first trip.

But on March 28, I landed in Vietnam, and we made the four-hour drive to Vinh Long. There we were led to an office and given a bottle of water. I had been awake for about twenty-eight hours and had not had a shower. But I remember looking out the door and seeing a woman carrying a little girl whom I immediately recognized from the picture on my computer. I suddenly understood how God adopts us as his own as I took Hannah in my arms and fell completely in love with her and in awe of God's promises. Paul says in Romans 8:16-17, "The Spirit himself testifies with our spirit that we are God's children. Now if we are children, then we are heirs—heirs of God and co-heirs with Christ, if indeed we share in his sufferings in order that we may also share in his glory."

On August 4, 2002, I stood before our church family and dedicated Hannah. The verse I chose for Hannah was 1 John 4:10: "This is love: Not that we loved God, but that he loved us and sent his Son as an atoning sacrifice for our sins." I chose this verse because I wanted Hannah to know what real love was—not my love but God's love. The pastor then asked our church family, "Do you promise to continue to pray for Susie and for Hannah as I know many have been doing over the last several months, and to provide good models for her as she has entered into a brand-new exciting and sometimes scary adventure of parenthood? Do you promise to pray for her and support her in any and every way that God may give you the opportunity to do so?" The pastor—yes, the same pastor who suggested I go to the personnel committee about adopting—then prayed that he was thankful that God was leading our congregation to be family to Hannah and to keep the promises that were made that day.

In 2005, I started the adoption journey again because I couldn't imagine Hannah growing up as an only child. So in September 2006, I brought Ella Phoung-Thao home from Ninh Thuan, Vietnam, at the age of twenty-one months. Again, I stood before our church family and dedicated Ella with awe, love, and wonder.

It is hard to balance being a mother and a minister. Both of my parents are deceased, and my siblings each live ten hours away from us. But our community of faith is our family. Hannah and Ella have church members who serve as grandparents, aunts, and uncles who take care of them while I am away at meetings and trips. There are men who step up to the plate to be "Dad" for my girls. I know they need a male influence in their lives, and I feel guilty sometimes that they don't have a father. I worry that they will seek negative ways to get male attention. But I also know that they have learned so much and have so many opportunities that they would have never had back in Vietnam. We try hard to retain some Vietnamese culture in their lives and are hoping to return to Vietnam for birth-land tours.

I continue to travel on mission trips and church-related trips. And even though I know that I am helping others and that my children are well cared for, it doesn't get any easier to leave them . . . for my children know what it is like for their mother not to come back. I recently left on a mission trip to Moldova, and Ella, now seven, got out of bed two nights before I left with tears running down her cheeks because she was afraid something would happen to me on my trip and I wouldn't come home.

Because I now serve as Minister of Missions instead of Minister of Youth, my children have watched me go to other countries to help others as well as helping children right in our hometown. At first I was concerned about emphasizing orphan ministry in our church as I felt people might think it was my own "soapbox." But after visiting two of the state-run orphanages in Moldova, I realized that it was okay for God to use my passion to lead our church toward orphan ministry.

Since I brought Hannah and Ella home, many more in our church have become involved in adoption, both domestic and international. Our church family is learning how important it is for orphaned children all over the world to have a mom or dad. Our church's passion has been intergenerational worship and service. But there are children all over the world who do not have that luxury. So, as result of my recent trip to Moldova, our mission committee kicked off an official orphan ministry where we will focus on the need for our families to adopt, provide funding for adoption, and invest in orphanages where adoption does not take place.

This fall, my job will lead me to Myanmar to visit an orphanage where our church hopes to invest our money and time, because the "religion that God our Father accepts as pure and faultless is this: to look after orphans and widows in their distress and to keep oneself from being polluted by the world" (Jas 1:27). The adoption journey God began in my life years ago now includes our whole church as well as children around the world and in our own backyards. The journey continues.

———◆◆◆———

Rev. Susie C. Reeder, *a Kentucky native, lives in Fayetteville, North Carolina, with her two children, Hannah and Ella. A graduate of the University of Kentucky, she also received a MDiv in Christian Education from the Southern Baptist Theological Seminary in Louisville, Kentucky. Susie has served on staff at Snyder Memorial Baptist Church for over seventeen years, serving first as Youth Minister and now as Missions/Education Minister. Susie loves reading, adventurous cooking, traveling, and being artistic.*

CHAPTER 15

SUMMER AND SACRAMENTS

Holly Sprink

It's summer. In the Sprink family, that means, "Mom, get your game face on. It doesn't matter what time you set your alarm for, we're going to *wake* you up. We're seven and four. We're ready for action. We're ready for fun. We're ready for sixteen-hour days filled with sunscreen, ice cream, and runs through the sprinkler. Mom, we've got a schedule to maintain, full of swim lessons, zoo visits, and backyard campouts. And just when you think you're spent, Mom, we'll let you fall into bed so we can do it all over again tomorrow. It's summer, Mom. It's go-time."

And I *love* go-time with my kiddos. I love the *together* of summer, and I realize I'm lucky. As a mother, cross-cultural worker, and writer, I look forward to summer, when lunches can be made and not packed ahead of time and when my car seems to drive itself to Sonic periodically for cherry limeades. Spontaneity rules in the summertime, and each spring I eagerly await the break from the routine.

Of course, that break in routine means a break in the carefully crafted family schedule, leading to my inevitable anxious question, "How will I get *my work* done?" Perhaps it's because of the age of my kids, perhaps it's this season of life, or perhaps it's just my sin, but I tend to compartmentalize my mommy tasks and my ministry tasks. Cognitively, I recognize how important both categories are, but in actuality, time spent balancing the family calendar feels like it should count for my daily workout. So every nine months as summer approaches, the white board is wiped clean and I attempt to fashion an incredible summer. I am hopelessly optimistic, but (maybe it's all the cherry limeades talking) I feel that surely this year I will be able to craft a summer with the perfect balance of family fun and mommy ministry.

Then the summer begins. We start out in a blaze of museum visits and library story times. We do craft and crayon time that sneakily reviews math facts and writing skills. And in the midst of all this fun, I realize that the writing time I'd carefully carved out during one child's nap and another child's reading hour has somehow vanished. Or I turn around and realize that the day I'd guarded to bake cookies with the kids and take them to visit our Somali friends got swallowed up in doctor's and dentist's appointments. Somewhere around July, my neat, compartmentalized categories of family and ministry have gone out the window right alongside the kids' bedtimes.

And while my naiveté may make you think otherwise, I've been working at this motherhood and ministry balance for a while now. I began to process motherhood and ministry issues from the get-go, as my last three months of seminary coincided with my first trimester of pregnancy. As so many others would say, motherhood has brought about a different level of self-awareness, and there are so many things I could write about here— not as an expert but as someone who is faced with the issues and questions consistently.

Questions and insecurities constantly arise, driven primarily by the season of life that I'm currently in: Am I a minister if I'm not currently on staff at a church? Am I seen as one, and does it bother me if I'm not? Will my daughter and son see a proper perspective on ministry and motherhood? How do we balance a family with a mother and father who are both ministers? Should we only work at churches and with people who affirm both of us in ministry? Will I get to be paid for the vocational work I do, or will I just need to get "a job" my whole life? Will I only be seen as the "lovely wife" and a great volunteer? Since I've been fortunate enough to get a degree, is it wrong for me *not* to work at this time?

Sometimes these questions arrive in my mind, settle in, and pass gently, like seasons. Sometimes they're more like a balloon that gets squeezed on one end, and there's a quick pop on the other. But probably the most consistent struggle I have is displayed most prominently in summertime, in the *practice* of the daily family routine. I'm happy with my choices in life and with our choices for our family. In my head, I believe in the union of faith and family, ministry and motherhood. But do I live it out in the midst of the routine?

Maintaining a proper perspective on that daily family routine and the "ministry stuff" in my schedule is my biggest living, breathing challenge.

You know what routine I'm talking about—the things in a family that need to be done every day, with no end in sight: the flossing, the food prep, the backpack checking, the bedtimes. If I'm honest with myself (and usually when I've let myself get too tired), these tasks become the checklist that I rush through *so that* I can get everyone out the door and get on with the "ministry tasks" I have before me. I've got English classes to teach, research to do for a chapter, and a friend to meet for marriage counseling, all before the bus drops the kids back home. But I am learning, as I live in the daily routine, to feel that union and lean into it a little further each day.

On my dresser, I have framed a quote by Denise Roy that reads, "Your hands are the hands of a mother, administering the sacrament of ordinary life" (*Momfulness* [San Francisco: Jossey-Bass, 2007] 130). This reminds me that the compartments I've set up are of my own doing, and, as such, unnecessary. It reconnects me to the reality that pigtails and peanut butter sandwiches may be the very grace I'm called to give that particular day.

Psalm 127:3-5 reads, "Don't you see that children are GOD's best gift, the fruit of the womb his generous legacy? Like a warrior's fistful of arrows are the children of a vigorous youth. Oh, how blessed are you parents, with your quivers full of children! Your enemies won't stand a chance against you; you'll sweep them right off your doorstep" (Eugene Peterson, *The Message*). I read this recently, and it gave me pause. I agreed with the first part: my kids are a priceless gift from God. But the second part made me think. My children are weapons? They'll protect me? From whom? From what?

And what I've found is this: that as I administer the sacraments of everyday life, I keep in mind that I am just as much in need of the wafer and the wine. I am not only the giver of grace; I am also the recipient. I need the grace of the routine of family life as much as the children do. It protects me, if only from myself.

Being someone who once tested off the chart on the introversion scale of a Myers-Briggs test, I could easily sit reading and writing all day. I could begin to believe that my own thought life and my own writing are, in actuality, how I always live. I could quickly become absorbed in my own ministry activities if I had endless time in which to do them. But the grace of the family routine enters, almost in a monastic sense, and helps me to find wholeness. For, when my time is limited, I recognize that God is the one at work—not me—and that his work will continue in all of his servants around the world. This properly shifts the focus away from me and centers it on God. Or, when I am interrupted by my kids and quickly lose my patience, I am reminded that a kind letter from a reader is meaningless if the ones who live in my own household can't see me living out what I'm writing. While I may not have a quiver full, as it says in Psalms, my seven-year-old Lucy and four-year-old Mikias are protective weapons indeed.

I've experienced ministry and motherhood in two different yet similar ways—through a birth child, Lucy, and through Mikias, adopted from Ethiopia at nineteen months of age. This, too, has been something of a sacrament in our lives, something that protects me from my Holly-centered view of American womanhood. I've found that this process has connected me to women and children I've never met: Habtu, for instance, an Ethiopian construction worker and Mikias's birth mom. I long to meet the God who saw to it that Holly and Habtu's lives were forever intertwined through the grace of Mikias. And through every random interruption—like when Mikias came up to me the other day while I was writing and said, "Hey, Mom, do you think I can blow this whistle for twenty-one hours? Watch me try . . . WHEEEEEEEE"—through *all* that, I am connected to other mothers all across the globe whose babies ride on their backs and go to work with them all day as well. As it says in Psalm 10, "orphans get parents, the homeless get homes . . . God's grace and order wins" (vv. 18, 16, *The Message*).

I find that this grace comes unexpectedly in the working-it-out, in the *living*-it-out. Recently, my family was at church on my husband Matt's day off, setting up for a weekend-long meal-packing event that would provide more than 40,000 meals to the horn of Africa for famine relief. On this particular Friday, Lucy and Mikias were doing their best to "help" and keep themselves occupied while we set up tables, scales, and fifty-pound bags of soy protein and dehydrated vegetables. While we were wading through the piles of supplies and trying to figure out the best ways for the assembly lines to work, our kids were bouncing balls around and lip-syncing on the stage to music playing over the sound system. It was not an ideal situation for anyone, but we were all trying to make it work (and frequent snacks helped as well).

As I unpacked the shipping labels, I began to ask myself once again whether I should just call a baby-sitter or take the children home. We were all doing our best to make the day go smoothly, but try as I might, I couldn't keep my meal packing from interrupting their kickball game. Mulling it over, I turned back to my labels, noticing that the meals were addressed to Bright Hope, a network of churches in Ethiopia that our church partnered with, and also the church that ran the orphanage Mikias came from. "Are these meals going to Bright Hope?" I asked Matt offhandedly. Yes, he said, Bright Hope would help with some of the distribution. And Mikias, who had been chasing a ball near me, paused and said cheerfully, "Oh, so that means some of this food is going to my birth mom."

And, once again, I am offered the wafer and the wine of ordinary life. I pray that I would administer it and accept it graciously in the unexpected, everyday places.

———————◆———————

*Rev. **Holly Sprink** received a BA in English from Baylor University and an MDiv from George W. Truett Theological Seminary. She is also the author of* Faith Postures: Cultivating Christian Mindfulness *and* Spacious: Exploring Faith and Place. *Holly enjoys working cross-culturally, writing, and experiencing the adventure of life with her husband Matt, daughter Lucy, and son Mikias. The Sprink family is at home in Blue Springs, Missouri.*

CHAPTER 16

MOM OR MINISTER?

Amy R. Stertz

I was thirty-seven weeks pregnant the first time I preached at my church. I knew how far along I would be in my pregnancy when I agreed to it. I also knew, as this was my first pregnancy, that I had no way to predict what would happen. Would I deliver early? Would I deliver late? Worst of all, would my water break in the middle of the sermon? I am still not quite sure why I agreed to preach so close to my due date, but nevertheless, on a hot July morning in summer 2008, I stood at the pulpit, nine months pregnant.

That morning, I prayed with and for our church, and I read and proclaimed the word of God, all while having contractions for the first time. The contractions turned out to be Braxton Hicks, and my daughter was not born for another two and a half weeks. But that morning I experienced in a real way the tension that I would live with as a mother and as a minister.

Even though the contractions were not a true signal of labor, the feelings and questions they brought up in me were very real. What was I getting myself into? Could I really do this? What was it going to be like? I had served in church ministry just long enough to have established a rhythm and routine that worked for me and my family. On the brink of becoming a mother, I knew that everything was going to change. I was going to have to relearn, revise, and renegotiate so much. In many ways, I felt like I was starting all over again. With each contraction, I felt completely overwhelmed and ill equipped for what lay ahead.

In July, I became mom to Sophie. In September, I became a working mom. I think I always knew I was meant to be a working mom. So far, it seems my hunch is right; I generally feel that I am a better mom because I am a working mom. Because I work, I tend to be more intentional about the time I spend with my husband and daughter. We have made family dinners a priority. Each weekend we go on an adventure. It may be to the library or the park in town, or it may be to the zoo or on a road trip to see family. Because I work, I tend to be more appreciative of and intentional about the time we have together.

I am fortunate that ministry is both flexible and family-friendly, so even though I am a working mom, I have also been able to be a hands-on mom. During Sophie's first two years, she was in the Parents' Day Out ministry at our church, which meant I was able to see and interact with her during my workday. Sophie was also able to spend time with me in my office in the afternoons when I didn't have someone else to watch her or on days when Parents' Day Out was closed.

Most working moms don't have a travel crib set up in their office; the fact that I did makes me incredibly grateful. And now that she is in a full-time program in town, I am still able to participate in their special class activities. I am fortunate that my job and my schedule are flexible enough that I can be more involved in Sophie's day-to-day activities than many working moms.

Ministry, by its nature, is family-friendly. So much of what I do in the church and in the community are things Sophie and I can do together. She has been to a volunteer appreciation banquet of a local nonprofit on whose board I serve. She has been to a Habitat for Humanity groundbreaking ceremony. She has been to numerous committee meetings at the church. Whenever an event is coming up, people will tell me to bring Sophie, and they are always excited to see her. My church family not only understands but also affirms my calling to be a mother.

The challenges of balancing the roles of full-time minister and hands-on mom have been significant. I have learned much that not only benefits me but also my family and my church. Working makes me a better mom; being a mom has made me a better minister. I have become more intentional about how I spend my time at work. I see a greater need and work toward establishing healthier boundaries in my relationships. I have had to face my limitations and make choices about how I use my time and energy. I am learning that I cannot do everything I want to do, and sometimes I cannot even do everything I should do. I have had to learn to say no, to ask for and accept help, and to make decisions about what is most important.

I have also struggled in my efforts to juggle the responsibilities of motherhood and ministry. I wrestle with doubt, stress, and feelings of inadequacy both at home and at work. I have missed time with my daughter because of meetings at church. I have missed newsletter deadlines because I was at the pediatrician's office. The pile of laundry to be done at home is as high as the pile of books and articles to read in my office. I can never seem to get everything done. As I try to honor one calling, I neglect the other.

When I was in divinity school, we talked about finding balance in ministry. Those were valuable conversations, and they seemed important then. But I was in my mid-twenties and a newlywed—two years shy of my first full-time ministry position and eight years shy of becoming a mother. The challenge of finding and creating balance now is an entirely different thing. These two callings, motherhood and ministry, are essential parts of my identity, and yet they overwhelm me.

In my first year as a mom, as I worked toward discovering some kind of balance, I took on the mantra, "If I feel like a bad mom and I feel like a bad minister at least once a day, then I'm doing something right." That was my way of finding balance in the midst of the chaos of my first year as a working mom. I cannot imagine not being a mother even as I cannot imagine not being a minister, but the weight of doing both at the same time can and has taken a toll on me. I often find that the two complement each other, but there are times when I feel stretched and I know one of them is not getting what it deserves.

When she was five months old, Sophie went through a terribly challenging period when sleep became an issue. She would wake up screaming every hour or two all through the night. This phase lasted for three months. I was so sleep deprived that I could barely function and my work suffered. When Sophie was just two, I spent seven days out of state at a Stephen Ministry Leader training course, leaving my husband and daughter behind during a snowstorm that kept them completely homebound for three days. It was hard enough not to be able to see my little girl for an entire week, but it was made even harder by not being able to offer support to my husband during a stressful situation at home.

Often, circumstances dictate where my time and energy go; but other times I feel like I have to choose between the two. This summer, after turning four, Sophie began to join me in the sanctuary for part of our worship service each Sunday. I find myself torn between the pulpit and the pew. I have a clear and specific calling to be in both places. I want very much to be the one who guides my daughter through worship, teaching her how to use a hymnal, when to stand, when to sit, how to give, and how to pray. But I am equally called to the platform and also desire to help my congregation encounter God through prayer and opening God's word. I struggle to know who I am first. Am I a mom or am I a minister? The reality is I am both.

I am aware that, because I am a minister, my daughter has experienced things the average four-year-old knows nothing about. Sophie has sat in on committee meetings, been with me at our local hospital to visit with church members, and spent her Saturday at the Salvation Army Kettle Cook-off. I hate that it is almost impossible for our family to take weekend trips as a family because my weekend schedule is a day off from that of my husband. Going to church on Sunday morning and Wednesday night isn't an option for us—it's a guarantee. Wednesdays were hard on Sophie when she was a baby and toddler. She would be tired and cranky when we got to church and often was such a mess by the time we left that I would plead with her to go to sleep in the car on the way home. Now she's enjoying Wednesday evening activities, but I know soon we will have to deal with homework assignments and schedule conflicts that will come with extracurricular activities.

I wonder and I worry what she will think about her childhood. Will she feel like it was normal? Will she resent me or the church because of the significant role it has played in our lives? I am well aware that her life and our schedules are different simply because she is the daughter of a minister.

I also struggle with how she perceives and will handle what ministry does to me. Most days I love it and it fulfills and energizes me, but some days I come undone and it gets the best of me. The work, the needs, the to-do list are just too much and I don't know what to do with myself, let alone her. On the bad days, I wonder if she should see and know how complicated and frustrating ministry can be. I want her to know of the joy it brings me, but I am not as sure about exposing her to the pain I experience at times. I am afraid of showing her that side of the church.

I want Sophie to understand that the church and its people are not perfect, but do I want her to know how imperfect they can be? The people in our church are her people as much as they are my people. I am not just a minister at a church; I am a minister at *her* church. I cannot separate or compartmentalize these two worlds; they are as much a part of her life as they are mine.

Despite the challenges, however, she has already begun to experience many positive things simply because her mom is a minister. Sophie is seeing the best of what church family is supposed to be. She is known by name. She is truly loved and deeply nurtured. Our church is full of men and women who will show up early and stay late to spend time with her while

I'm in a meeting or cleaning up after our Wednesday evening Bible study. Sophie and I have prepared meals together for families in our church, and she has feasted on food prepared for our family by other church members. She knows I visit people in the hospital just like people came to visit her in the same hospital when she was born. We read Bible stories, sing songs, and say prayers at home that she also hears in Sunday school, Preschool Musicians, and worship.

Sophie is experiencing the power and beauty of being part of a church family. While I worry about how much the church demands of her and takes from her, I am beyond grateful for all it gives her. Being the daughter of a minister means that she gets the best of what the church has to offer. Working for a church means that I have the support and affirmation of hundreds of people who genuinely care for my family and me.

As I stood at the pulpit feeling the contractions of new life that July morning, I had no idea of the life, joy, and hope that would be birthed in me as I became a mother. I had no idea how becoming a mother would make me a better minister. I had no idea how being a minister would make me a better mother. I may have more questions and doubts now than I did then, but I am incredibly grateful for the gift of grace that is mine by being able to serve faithfully in these two roles to which I have been called.

***

Rev. Amy R. Stertz has a Bachelor of Social Work from Mars Hill College and a Master of Divinity from the Campbell University Divinity School. She currently serves as the Associate Pastor in Christian Education at First Baptist Church in Aiken, South Carolina, and has previously served churches in Virginia and North Carolina. She is married to Joe and mother to Sophie. If she had free time, Amy would spend it traveling, reading, watching football, and spending time with family.

Chapter 17

Pregnant and Remembered Hopes

Meredith J. Stone

Pregnant with Hope

Church people love pregnant women at Christmas time. There's something about that big round belly that makes people smile and think of poor Mary on a donkey with the Savior growing inside her. I am familiar with this phenomenon because my two daughters were both born in February, which means I was big and pregnant during the Christmas seasons of 2003 and 2007.

When I was pregnant with my first daughter, I was working on a Master's degree and my husband was serving on a church staff in a small rural community. As the minister's spouse, who also happened to identify myself as a called minister, I sought ways to be a part of the ministry of the church in whatever place was open to me. One of those places in that particular church was the worship ministry. So in 2003 on the Sunday before Christmas, I was asked to pull my massively pregnant self up the stairs to the platform during the service, read Mary's song in Luke 1:46-55, and then sing a solo. In other words, I was asked to be the surrogate Mary.

While the service that day didn't include an examination of what being birth-er and nurturer to the Christ-child meant, the people in that church were given a meaningful snapshot of Jesus' mother. Sometimes Jesus' miraculous birth makes us forget about the tangible details. Jesus was an actual human being who grew inside of a woman. Mary did carry him in her belly for nine months, and he grew from tiny embryo to fetus inside of her. She had to think about what she ate and the activities she engaged in so that she could be sure to nurture this tiny creature into a fully functioning human being. Mary's womb was the first minister to the Christ as it provided a place for the baby human Jesus to grow.

Too often we only see Mary at the beginning or end of her pregnancy—receiving the message of Gabriel or on the donkey riding toward the stable behind that fateful inn. But we must remember that there was also an important middle part of her journey. There was a moment when the pregnant woman sang. While Mary's womb ministered and the fetus progressed, we get a snapshot of the pregnant Mary through the words of her song. Now, unlike me, she may not have been massively pregnant yet and she may not have had to stand on top of a platform to sing in front of a congregation, but in Luke 1 we see this marvelous picture of the pregnant Mary singing amid the difficulties in her life. Facing ridicule and being ostracized from her community, she sang. Entering into the unknown and being unsure of who would stand beside her, she sang. With God literally growing inside of her uterus, Mary sang and proclaimed to all who might listen the power, mercy, and justice of God.

It was with this picture of the pregnant Mary that I approached my second pregnancy-filled Christmas season in 2007. But my life was a little different in 2007. I was serving on a local church staff as a teaching pastor, and one of my responsibilities was to coordinate worship and preach during Advent. So when one of the lectionary passages for the third Sunday of Advent that year was Luke 1:46-55, I knew that, again, I brought a unique perspective into reading Mary's song.

As I read and reread Mary's song that week in preparation for Sunday, I felt a strong connection to her. I imagined her looking just like me—gigantic belly and all. I envisioned her responding to each kick and punch of the baby in her womb by placing her hand on her belly. And as her hand rose and fell with the movements of her unborn child, I wondered what she thought about and how she pictured that little person growing inside of her. Being almost eight months pregnant myself, at that point my imagination had constructed a detailed vision of who my second daughter would be. How did Mary picture her son, and what did she dream for him?

Then, as I read through commentaries and articles about Mary and her song for my sermon preparation, I began to see her mother's dream unfold in the words of Luke 1:46-55. Mary dreamed about the new world her son would bring into being. It would be a world where the poor, the downtrodden, and the powerless are restored. It would be a world where the strong, the rich, and the proud no longer dominate, but the lowly are lifted up and the hungry are fed—where God fills, helps, remembers, and is merciful by turning the entire order of society upside down. It would be a world where her son starts a revolution.

And there she sat.

Pregnant.

With the hope of a revolution of justice and redemption inside of her.

And with the expectation that she would *deliver* that hope to the world.

Looking down at my own pregnant belly, I was reminded that Mary was not the only one pregnant with that same kind of hope.

So when I preached that December morning in 2007, I tried to paint a picture of Mary that is sometimes forgotten—the Mary in-between Gabriel's visit and the manger. I attempted to use her pregnancy to illustrate the kind of hope we should all have. When we hope for redemption and justice, we should have Mary's kind of hope. It should be a hope that is assured since we can feel it kicking and punching and growing inside of us. It should be a hope that is active since, like labor and delivery, bringing our hope to fulfillment is not a passive endeavor.

And you can only imagine the congregational gasps as I said, "In fact, who better than Mary to illustrate to us the fact that we are all humble virgins whom God has impregnated with hope? That's right, you heard me—I'm not the only pregnant one in the room anymore. As followers of Christ, we have all been made pregnant by God's hope, and like Mary we have the privilege of giving birth to God's revolution of justice!"

After church that day, one male member of the congregation said to me, "I will never forget today—the day you made us all pregnant."

Now surely a male preacher could have preached the same sermon, or at least a sermon with the same message. Of the articles I read that week, which talked about the Mary inside all of us,[1] pregnancy metaphors for hope,[2] and Mary as the church's first theologian,[3] some were even written by men. But I imagine there was something about a large pregnant woman preaching from the pulpit and declaring everyone pregnant that might have caught everyone's attention. And in that moment, motherhood and ministry were a divine duet singing a lovely tune to the melody of Mary's song.

But more than that male church member had some insight into the meaning of the sermon that day. My older daughter, who was three at the time, was also in the church service to hear Mary's song. She sat on the back pew with my husband, James (side note: the back pew is a wonderful place for a three-year-old preacher's daughter who has a little trouble being quiet and still). And that morning while I was waving my arms around and moving back and forth at the front of the church, perhaps a little more animated than usual, I caught a glimpse of her. She wasn't coloring, eating a snack, or "reading" a book like she usually did. She was standing on that pew waving her own arms around and mimicking my every movement. When the service was over, I went back to her and asked, "What were you doing on the pew back here, sweetheart?"

And she replied, "I want to be a preacher just like you mommy."

That morning, she also saw Mary's hope—a hope that would turn the world upside down: when big pregnant women can preach about the theological meaning of an expectant hope, and little girls can dream about being a preacher just like mommy.

Remembering Hope

About a year and a half after that divine Sunday morning filled with hope, I found myself losing that sense of pregnant expectation.

When I became pregnant with our youngest, I expected that my life would pretty much continue as it had been. The church I was serving was a smaller church, so my role as teaching pastor was only paid as part-time. Therefore, I had another part-time job doing seminary admissions, which helped to pay for my ministry habit. So when the youngest was born, the plan was that I would continue to serve in both capacities, and my sweet new daughter would go to day care just as her older sister did.

But things do not always go as planned.

At first, it seemed like our second child was simply a bit more prone to getting sick than other kids. And essentially, that is all it was. But she also didn't get better as fast as other kids did. What we didn't realize was that this meant any and every illness escalated quickly. Sinus and ear infections meant 105-degree fevers, secondary illnesses, and massive amounts of antibiotics, which in turn led to vomiting, a failure to thrive, more hospital visits, lots of tests, and surgeries.

When she was eighteen months old, we finally saw an immune system specialist who told us that he couldn't find anything in her immune system that he could fix, but it obviously was not as strong as other kids'. Failure to thrive, though, is a major issue for a tiny eighteen-month-old. His suggestion: take her out of day care and remove her from any situation where she would be exposed to illnesses. Translation: give up the fulfillment of your calling that you had prayed for and desired so long.

Until then, none of her doctors had given us directives that we had to do this. But after the fifth doctor, our pediatrician, finally succumbed and made the same suggestion, we knew the time had come to make difficult decisions.

I have no regrets that I decided to leave my local church position. But having no regrets is not the same as having no pain. It is difficult to describe the sense of loss I felt. Several months later we began attending another church, and I had a hard time not crying every Sunday afternoon. I missed church ministry. I missed living my life in relational ministry with a congregation I served. It destroyed me to think that my youngest would never stand on a back pew and dream of being a preacher like mommy. But most of all, I missed feeling like I was doing what I was created to do.

But in the midst of the pain, I regularly reminded myself that I was created to do more than ministry. The same God who had created me and called me to be a minister had also created and called me to be a mother. It's not that I had ever forgotten or neglected my call to motherhood; it was just easier to balance a co-calling to motherhood and ministry before one of those callings was in crisis. Slowly, I learned to trust that God was not going to abandon the call to ministry He had placed on my life simply because there was a moment when my calling to motherhood needed to become my sole focus.

One day balance would return, and my co-calling could resume its rhythm in the divine duet. So I returned to Mary. And I remembered her hope.

Mary dreamed of a revolution of justice—a world turned upside down. And Mary's role, the way that Mary got to participate in that revolution, was not just through giving birth to the one who would bring it about, but also through taking care of that child. Each time Mary fed and bathed baby Jesus, she contributed to God's merciful purpose. Each time she wiped toddler Jesus' nose, she joined in God's intent for redemption and revolution. She didn't lose her hope because there was nurturing to be done once he was born; she cared for him and cultivated him so that her desire and hope for justice could come to fruition.

So feeding, bathing, and wiping noses became the way I participated in God's purposes. One little human being needed a revolution of God's mercy in that moment. And like Mary had been for Jesus, I had been created to be the one who nurtured the hope growing inside of her.

But now, turning to today, as all the doctors had promised, my sweet daughter has almost completely outgrown her chronic issues. And the God I had to learn to trust has been faithful to the co-calling on my life. My divine duet has resumed. While the melody is not the same as before, I hope that the complexity has made its harmonies all the richer in tone. I hope that, like Mary, I understand more deeply not only how to birth hope but also to nurture it to maturity. I hope that one day my children read this and realize the fullness of understanding they have brought to my life as a minister.

But while my pregnant and remembered hopes are many, one of my hopes has already been fulfilled. This summer my youngest finally got her chance to hear mom preach. And even though it was from the nursery and not the back pew, I was told that she watched on the television feed and stood with her arms outstretched and proclaimed to everyone how Moses was going to make sure that the fire in the tree didn't kill everyone so that they could all go to heaven. Oh, to be a four-year-old preacher.

Notes

1. Ronald Goetz, "The Mary in Us All," *Christian Century* 104/37 (December 1987): 1108–1109.

2. Nancy D. Becker, "Mary's Hope and Our Hope," *Christian Century* 100/35 (November 1983): 1072; Carol Gilbertson, "Advent's Pregnant Watch," *Currents in Theology and Mission* 27/6 (December 2000): 453–56.

3. Patrick D. Miller, "Mary: The Church's First Theologian," *Theology Today* 56/3 (October 1999): 293–96.

Rev. Meredith J. Stone serves as women in ministry specialist for Texas Baptists. Her work includes resourcing and supporting women serving in vocational ministry across Texas and consulting with churches and institutions that support women in leadership. Meredith is also working on a PhD in Biblical Interpretation through Brite Divinity School at Texas Christian University. Meredith's husband, James, serves as Director of Church Relations for Hardin-Simmons, and they have two daughters, Hallie and Kinsey, who are nine and five.

CHAPTER 18

THE PHOTOGRAPH

Melanie Kilby Storie

I have this photograph. A classroom of children in the middle of their school day pose with their limbs at wild angles. Their pants have begun to look rumpled, and their shirts show evidence of what they ate for lunch. Each face shines with excitement in the flash of the camera. A moment of silly joy caught forever. There may be hundreds of thousands of photographs like it all over the world, but this one is particularly special to me. There is only one white face in this group of bubbly first graders. He stands beside a black boy, his friend. They each have an arm around the other. Their free hands each wield a peace sign. That white boy in the picture is my son, Aidan. His friend is James. This is the story of how they came to have their arms around each other, and how my son and I learned what it means to live at peace with one another.

My husband and I moved to Perry County, Alabama, with our two young boys in 2008 to work with an organization called Together for Hope, a partnership of the Cooperative Baptist Fellowship with twenty of the poorest counties in the United States. Perry County is a rural area south of Birmingham and not too far from Selma. The population of this area is eighty percent African American and twenty percent white. The majority of the people living in Perry County are descended from slaves and from those who were on the front lines of the Civil Rights movement. Unfortunately, many people in the county are extremely poor. Our job was to get to know people in Perry County, learn from them, be the presence of Christ, and work alongside them to build up the positive assets of the community.

We prepared our children as best as we could for this change. We were moving from Roanoke, Virginia, where my children had been exposed to a variety of people and cultures, to an area where they would be in the minority. I didn't want them to be afraid to make new friends. I told them about Ruby Bridges, a black girl who was Aidan's age when she bravely went to a new school where she didn't look like everyone else.

Aidan, who was about to begin first grade, asked, "Will I be the only white boy in my class?"

I told him that there would probably be other white children.

We bought school supplies. We bought navy and khaki pants and collared shirts for his school uniform. We sent Aidan to school the first day, and I held my breath a little.

He came home and seemed to be just fine. He liked his teacher and lunch. But as the sun set and the supper dishes were put away, I began to ask him about new friends. Aidan said he made a few, but then he dropped a bombshell.

"A boy called me a name because I'm white."

I felt my ears ring and my face go white. A sort of "Mama Bear" anger began to rise up in my throat. I wanted to call the teacher or a parent. I wanted to get in the car and head back to Roanoke. But a sane woman was living somewhere in my body. I took a deep breath, choked "Mama Bear" back down, and asked Aidan to tell me what name the boy called him. I gritted my teeth and prepared for the worst.

"*Stupid.* James called me *stupid.*"

After a quick mental review of the racial slurs I knew, I was sure that "stupid" wasn't one of them. I sighed in relief and asked Aidan to tell me what happened.

To assess what the children knew, the teacher asked the class to write their numbers from one to one hundred. Aidan was proud that he was the first in the class to finish. He stood up to take his paper to the teacher. The teacher complimented Aidan and he proudly returned to his seat across from James, who called Aidan "stupid." And in our house at that time, "stupid" was pretty much the worst word a person could say.

Aidan continued to tell me that James was the last to finish his numbers. In fact, he didn't finish at all. He couldn't even write up to twenty. James made a big impression on Aidan and not just because of the name-calling. James also had a hard time sitting still. He was in trouble most of the day. He was mean. A bully, according to Aidan. In addition, Aidan told us that he was the only white person in his class. We had learned that most white families sent their children to a private school. We now knew that "most" was all but four or five children in a school of over three hundred. (Our son, Owen, would later enter the Head Start preschool in town, a wonderful program in which he too was the only white child.)

I felt terrible that I had led Aidan to believe he would share the same skin color with at least one or two other children in his class. I was sorry that James called him a name in front of the class, making Aidan feel even more singled out. But I also felt sad for James. James, who couldn't write his numbers and stayed in trouble all day. So Aidan and I decided to pray for James. We prayed that God would help James to be kind, to "make good choices" as we so often say in our house. For two weeks, we prayed, and I listened to more "James" stories each day when Aidan came home. After that first day, James picked on Aidan no more or less than anyone else in class. Aidan was making friends and settling in. I worried more about him feeling like a sore thumb than he ever did, so I let Aidan teach me a thing or two about going with the flow for a change.

A few weeks into the school year, I began to volunteer in Aidan's class. The first day I walked in, the teacher pulled me aside and pointed out James. In a classroom in one of the poorest counties in the United States, James was one of the poorest students. He was one of eight children living in a small trailer. His mother tried to provide for him and his siblings, but with no jobs in the area, she relied mostly on a small welfare check. His clothes were dirty, his pants too short. It was difficult to understand him when he talked. He was behind in reading, in math, in everything. But James had one of the most beautiful smiles and a boyish mischievousness I recognized from my own boys. I asked the teacher if I could work with James. She was skeptical. She shared that James had a lot of anger bottled up. She didn't want me to try only to get discouraged when I could help other children who might be more receptive. I understood where she was coming from, but I still wanted to try. She reluctantly agreed.

Over the next weeks and months, James became my friend, and more important, I earned his trust and friendship. We sat on the floor with flash cards of his sight words, and I told him he could hold on to the ones he knew. He wanted to make his pile of cards higher than mine. When he got frustrated, I Frisbee-flicked the words he knew at him one by one until he laughed, collapsing onto his side in a joyous heap. The other children in the class began to trickle over to our game and cheer for James when he read the words correctly.

Aidan's classmates would often greet me with hugs in a great mass of excitement as I entered the room. At first, James would hang back. So after making sure to give a squeeze to Aidan, I headed straight for James. I'd pat his shoulder or rub his head until, one day, he turned and gave me a great bear hug.

Another day, I came a little early and the children were lined up in the hallway, coming in from lunch. I noticed one girl's shoe was untied, so I bent to tie it. Out of the corner of my eye, I saw James bend down and untie his shoe. He stood back up and waited for me to come to him, to spend a moment tying his shoes. I felt like I was doing something holier than tying a shoe, like I was washing his feet. But in so many ways, he was washing mine.

Aidan told me at home that James was his friend now, that all that praying had made James nicer. Maybe it did. But maybe those prayers opened our eyes a little wider too, so that we could both see James a little more clearly.

The next school year, James wasn't in Aidan's class, but I made sure to seek him out every time I was at school. We began a pen pal program with the children in Perry County and children back at partnering churches in North Carolina and Virginia. I printed cards for each child to write a little something about themselves: favorite color, hobbies, and on one line "What I like most about myself." I loved looking through the cards when they were complete and pairing the child with a pen pal. I will never forget seeing James's card and reading what he wrote. Under "What I like most about myself," James wrote, "I have learned to read." I was so proud of him, as proud as I would have been had he been my own child.

One day that first-grade year, I brought my camera to school. I asked the children to get together. I wanted a picture of them. As any mother of a first grader can tell you, getting a few together to stand still for a picture is improbable. Getting an entire classroom to do so is next to impossible, so I told them to act like they loved each other and get a little crazy. In that photograph, hands are on hips and in the air. Gap-toothed grins are the norm, not the exception. Mouths are open. Eyes are crossed. And two boys stand, their arms around each other, their hands proclaiming peace. Let it be so.

———◆◆◆———

Rev. Melanie Kilby Storie is a graduate of Catawba College and Campbell University Divinity School. While in seminary, Melanie married Matthew Storie, served as a youth and children's minister, had a son (Aidan, 11), and finally graduated while eight months pregnant with her second son (Owen, 8). Melanie has served churches in North Carolina and Virginia as Minister of Children. Recently, she served with the Cooperative Baptist Fellowship in Alabama. Melanie currently lives in Independence, Virginia.

CHAPTER 19

GRACE AND HOPE

Virginia Ross Taylor

I like to think of both motherhood and ministry as callings. But just because you are called to something doesn't mean it's going to be easy. Neither my journey to motherhood nor my journey to ministry were without obstacles, setbacks, or heartbreaks.

My calling to motherhood is deep-rooted. I am the oldest child in my family and spent most of my childhood mothering (they would say, "bossing") my younger brothers and sisters. My calling became clear when my husband and I were dating and I realized that I wanted him to be the father of my children. We were young and not quite ready to start a family, but we knew that was something we wanted together.

We had been trying to get pregnant for many months when my mother called me on my twenty-fifth birthday to tell me that she was going to have a baby. I was happy for her (and slightly embarrassed), and even though her pregnancy shined a spotlight on the fact that I wasn't pregnant, it also gave me hope. If my mom could get pregnant and carry a baby to full-term in her forties, then there was still plenty of time for me to have a baby.

But it was not easy. Both my husband and I had to endure many tests, and both of us had to have surgery before it was all over. And then there were all the well-meaning friends and families inquiring about our plans to start a family *soon*. If only we knew when it would happen! The pressure we were putting on ourselves and the stress of the situation became almost unbearable.

And then the day came when our hopes were realized and our prayers were answered: we were pregnant! We were like the man Jesus healed, telling everyone our news, even strangers (Mark 1:40-45). But that happiness was short-lived. I miscarried during the first trimester. I suppose that could have made me angry with God, but I had a real peace that could have only come from God, so all was well.

We were able to put the idea of having a baby on the back burner for a while. It was during this time that I experienced a call to ministry. I talked with my pastor, and he was supportive and encouraged me to go through the ordination process. Looking back, I had no idea what I was doing—except that I knew God had called me and that seemed to be enough.

Part of my calling was to go to seminary, which meant a cross-country move for us. I really did not want to go to a Baptist seminary because that was during the height of the controversy over women in ministry in the Southern Baptist Convention. I didn't want to spend any of my time in seminary defending something I couldn't help or do anything about. I was called and I was a woman, and nothing would change either of those things.

Seminary was a wonderful time. I loved all of my classes and enjoyed the companionship I shared with my classmates and professors. It was a dream. Right in the middle of that dream I woke up to find out I was pregnant again. We were excited but also terribly nervous. I spent the entire pregnancy waiting for something bad to happen, but it never did. And during the first week of classes in the fall term, I gave birth to a healthy and beautiful baby girl. We named her Grace.

None of this went according to my plans, but I welcomed the detour. I was able to take classes the next semester, just not as many. It was during this time that my husband learned that his job was ending, which meant another cross-country move and leaving seminary before I finished my degree. I found out that I would be able to complete my requirements at another seminary, and that made it a lot easier to make the move. Six years and several ministry positions later, I finally completed my seminary degree. By this time, Grace was eight years old.

Up until this point, I had been serving as a minister to college students and felt fulfilled in my ministry. I thought I would be a college minister my entire ministry. But that, too, didn't go according to plan.

As a church staff member, I would get the opportunity to preach a couple of times each year. Those experiences, along with my preaching classes, made me start to think of myself as a "preacher" in addition to being a "minister."

Over a short period, a restlessness began to rise up inside me that initially took the form of "sermon critic." I listened to the Scripture read in morning worship and immediately begn to hear the many ways it might speak to the congregation. Then I would listen to the sermon and note the things that worked and the things that didn't work: illustrations, length, flow, applications. Around this time, I began asking my pastor if I could preach for him when he was going to be away on vacation or had other things going on. But the invitation never came.

All the while, this call to preach was growing stronger and stronger. I went to my pastor to talk with him about my call, and he suggested that I consider changing denominations. "Odds are," he said, "you are not going to find a Baptist church that will call a woman preacher." I knew he was right, but it made me heartsick to think about it. In the meantime, I reminded him that I would be happy to preach for him any time he needed pulpit supply. Truth be told, I practically begged him for opportunities to preach, but to no avail.

In the in-between time, I began to question and doubt my preaching. Maybe he didn't want me to preach because he didn't think I was good enough. Perhaps he didn't let me preach because he or the church didn't think women should be preachers. I certainly wasn't feeling affirmed and encouraged as a preacher, and despite the tugging in my soul, I questioned my calling.

And then the phone call came. But it wasn't the pastor; it was the minister of music. He called me at home to tell me that the pastor was going to be away the next week (I was beginning to get excited) and had asked the minister of music to preach. The minister of music was calling to ask if I would be willing to do the children's sermon.

I later wrote the pastor an e-mail describing this moment as being hit in the head with a two-by-four. I finally got it: he wasn't going to let me preach. He pretty much admitted that was true.

In order to prove my willingness to serve, I agreed to do the children's sermon that Sunday, and I did it well. Actually, I probably overdid it. But that doesn't matter. What matters is that when the minister of music got up to preach that day, the first words out of his mouth were, "I don't know why [the pastor] asked me to preach today, because I'm not a preacher." And his sermon affirmed that his calling was to be a music minister, not a preacher.

I was still wallowing in self-pity, thinking I must be a pretty bad preacher if my pastor chose this guy to preach over me, when my daughter came up to me right after the service (she had been sitting with the youth in the balcony). Grace said, "When [the minister of music] started off his sermon that way, I said to myself, 'I sure am glad I can't see my mom's face right now.'"

And with those words, my then thirteen-year-old daughter freed me to be angry—not sorry for myself but *angry* that my pastor would treat me that way. Once I saw her anger, I couldn't allow him to continue. If not for myself, I had to do it for my daughter.

Augustine wrote, "Hope has two beautiful daughters. Their names are anger and courage; anger at the way things are, and courage to see that they do not remain the way they are" (in Robert McAfee Brown, *Spirituality and Liberation: Overcoming the Great Fallacy* [Louisville: Westminster Press, 1988] 136). My beautiful daughter helped me embrace the anger I felt at the way things were and gave me the courage to make sure they didn't stay that way.

A year later, I was in conversation with another denomination to obtain a privilege of call when a Baptist church in our city called me to be their pastor and preacher. *A Baptist church in our city called me to be their pastor and preacher.* That's more than a fourteen-word sentence: it is a gift of grace from God—much like my daughter, Grace.

Instead of seeing me silenced, my daughter was able to see that God gave me a voice and a place to use that voice. She was proud that her mom was a preacher. She even said that she wanted to make a book of my sermons so that she would have them to show to her children one day (my best compliment ever).

Most of all, I hope she has seen that God has given her a voice. God will give her a place to use that voice, no matter what her calling. And when she does experience obstacles, setbacks, and heartbreaks, she will know that the hope she has been given will give her the anger *and* courage she needs to keep going.

Rev. Virginia Ross Taylor was the first woman pastor of Lystra Baptist Church in Chapel Hill, North Carolina, and currently serves as a freelance minister. She has a Master of Divinity from Fuller Theological Seminary in Pasadena, California. She and her husband, Ralph, are the parents of one grown daughter, Grace, a psychology major at the University of North Carolina, Asheville.

CHAPTER 20

"THAT'S LIFE!"

Kristin Adkins Whitesides

The first time my four-year-old climbed onto the platform and sat on my lap, my senior pastor was only going through the opening announcements. We had not yet had our musical time of preparation or call to worship. So it felt okay that Isaac had escaped from my husband and shimmied into my lap and was sitting there, quietly waiting for us to go and greet the congregation together.

My husband was busy, after all. He was sitting on the front pew with all the other parents, jiggling our four-month-old, Samuel, on his knee as we waited for the parent-child dedication that would come later in the service. Samuel was happy. He was eagerly trying to interact with another baby who was sitting on her mother's lap, studiously ignoring him and looking saintly and angelic in her ruffles.

Isaac was full of nerves. He, somewhat ironically, had been nervous about getting up in front of the congregation as we dedicated his brother. He was also unsure how he felt about all eyes being on his Samuel and all the attention and sweetness that would be directed toward this new little interloper in his life. Wrapped up in all of it was excitement and pride that he was a new big brother and was ready to pledge to help teach Samuel about God's love. So he climbed into my lap. For affirmation. For affection. For security. All the reasons any young child might climb into his mother's arms.

I, too, was a pile of nerves. I was silently communicating with my husband through raised eyebrows, quirked lips, and weird attempts at telepathy about how he ought to hold the baby, restrain the preschooler, and try to act like he was enjoying the whole endeavor. I wanted to be on the front pew. I wanted to be holding my children. Why was I up on the platform? Oh. That's right. I am one of the pastors. So we needed this to go perfectly.

After all, if the pastor can't get her own kids to behave and enjoy being in church, what hope does she have of leading anyone else?

After our time of greeting, I firmly told Isaac to remain with his daddy while I returned to the platform to lead our call to worship. I assured him that I would join him right after I was finished. He nodded solemnly. I shot a pleading look at my husband, who shrugged his shoulders, signaling that he would try his best, and then I made my way back to the platform. Isaac sat quietly through the instrumental meditation. But as I stood up to begin the call to worship, he scrambled up the side of the platform and plastered himself to my leg.

Still, that would have been fine. It was fine. Until he found something of interest on one of the shelves in the pulpit, which he began to reach for. I had to sort of sweetly shove him back to my side. He then began tugging on my hand and broke loose, moving toward the opposite edge of the platform. Taking advantage of the litany-style call to worship, I let the congregation begin their response as I marched over to Isaac, picked him up, and carried him back to the platform. He pulled the foam off the microphone. Reaching the last lines of the litany, I said an impromptu and very vigorous "Amen!" and carried him off the platform down to the front pew as the first strains of the hymn of praise began. Did I mention it was Mother's Day?

This is the two-edged sword of motherhood and ministry. We are infinitely blessed as our children are held and nurtured by a community of faith. We are blessed as we are able to involve them actively in our work and our calling. We are blessed with the fluidity and flexibility of a job that is also a way of life. And yet, the same blessings can seem like a curse when there is a toddler tantrum in the middle of a covered dish dinner. Any normal mother would simply pick up her child and leave. But if it is your job to be at the covered dish dinner, you simply have to manage as best you can and fall apart later. Women who are leading meetings in boardrooms rarely have their children playing with blocks in the corner. Women who are doctors are rarely seen chasing their preschoolers through the halls of their offices. And yet, for better or worse, this can be the life of a mother in ministry.

Parenting in public is never easy. For pastors, it can be compounded by unrealistic visions, whether they are your own misplaced expectations or those of your congregation, of the minister who has the perfect family: all the children are neatly dressed, smiling, and engaged, well-versed in all the important Bible stories, with nary a hair out of place.

Sadly, or perhaps thankfully, that vision is never met in reality. Now is the time to set it aside for a fuller vision of incarnational ministry. While we are never called, even partially, to be God, we are, in all reality, called to be *fully human*. That means that sometimes we will fall off the balance beam between mother and minister and feel like we are doing neither well. That means that sometimes we may have spit-up on the shoulders of our suits when we step into the pulpit to preach. That means we will be just like the rest of our congregation: flawed, harried, human, and wholly loved by God.

If we live into this reality, this incarnational ministry, perhaps we can begin creating a new model of what it means to pastor a congregation well. It will mean learning to do a few things that are rarely talked about in seminary: naming what you and your family need, learning to accept help, and being able to laugh and show grace to your children and yourself. The first two skills are not widely touted as pastoral gifts. However, learning how to name what we need in order to function as whole people and as parents will perhaps be the most important lesson we can learn in ministry.

Perhaps this is asking for or creating a modified work schedule so that you can pick up your kids from school. Perhaps it is having your infant with you in the office. Perhaps it is sending a committee report with a colleague and missing the meeting because it coincides with bedtime routines. I have done all of these things. It is important to ask: what will allow me to be both a good parent and a good pastor? Once we decide what that looks like, it is important to ask for what we need in order to fill both roles well.

Certainly there will be moments of chaos. There are always times when we feel as though we are managing to let everyone down and pleasing no one, least of all ourselves. And yet, if we simply learn to ask for what we need, we have taken the first step toward embracing our lives of ministry and motherhood for what they are: lives. Not balancing acts. Not performances. Not schedules or routines or checklists. But lives that move through seasons of needs and desires like anyone else's. If we can learn to ask for what we need in order to live our lives well and fully, we will be much less begrudging of others who ask us to help them cope with the personal needs they, too, face. We will also be modeling what it looks like to face the needs of our lives with realistic eyes and with plans of action and care. These are important lessons to learn for our own well-being, as well as important lessons for our congregation to learn through our example.

Of course, it is no good to ask for what we need if we are not also willing to accept help. This is, for many of us, the hardest lesson to learn. As pastors we are taught to be fixers and helpers for others. It is an uncomfortable and vulnerable place to have to ask for and accept help from others. It must be done in a context of trust and healthy relationships. But when done well, it, too, can be a model for what it means to be a person of faith.

Too often our congregations are led to believe that people of faith must have it all together before they enter the doors of the church. Pastors who keep up the charade of perfection only reinforce this lie. If we are fully human and learn to accept help when it is offered and when it is needed, we will find grace upon grace. In Ephesians we read that it is the job of the pastor to equip Christians to do ministry. How arrogant of us to assume that those ministries will never be directed back toward us!

During both of my pregnancies, I faced complications that forced me to be on bed rest for extended periods. My first reaction was to turn off the phone and wallow in my discomfort, fear, and feelings of helplessness. However, my wonderful senior pastor, ministerial staff, and congregation would simply not leave me alone. Week after week they brought us meals every other day. During my second pregnancy, members took care of my preschooler, offering to watch him so my husband could take a break. Friends came and brought lunch and ate with me. I was served bedside Communion. I was served fried chicken. My nails were painted and magazines were shared. One day one of my youth leaders and her teenage daughter came and folded laundry and cleaned our kitchen. The men's Sunday school class sent me beautiful flowers. My senior pastor called, came by, and made sure to keep me in the loop about what was going on in the office. He also refused to engage with me in talks about docking pay or a leave of absence. I worked from home as best I could from a laptop and cell phone and was assured daily of the ways that I was loved and cared for by God and by my church.

This is not always how the story goes. Perhaps that is why I so treasure the gifts I was offered by my congregation during those difficult months. Being vulnerable is never the preferred status—for anyone. And yet we all will be vulnerable either privately or publicly at some point in our ministry.

Becoming a parent makes one vulnerable in new and sometimes terrifying ways. We are no longer completely in control of our bodies. We are certainly not completely in control of the little humans who become part of our lives. What a gift it is when a congregation is allowed to and wants to care for their pastor and her family. And if we are able to open ourselves up, even in our vulnerability, we can receive an even greater gift when we learn to accept the care and love and help that is offered.

How I wish I had taken my own advice on that Mother's Day. I spent time picking out Samuel's dedication outfit. I talked with Isaac about what it meant for us to pledge to raise him to know God's love. I made sure we all ate a good breakfast. And then I left my husband stranded on the front pew wrangling two squirming boys on his own. We should have thought about what we would need: extra hands. And then we should have asked for them and accepted the offers. It would have been easy to ask a church friend to sit with the boys to keep Isaac occupied and help my husband juggle. Plenty of people would have been happy to help. Instead, I spent the rest of my Mother's Day mortified by my son's behavior and worried about how my congregation would perceive me as a pastor and a mother. I was too distracted even to enjoy or delight in Samuel's dedication.

I should have named what I needed and accepted some help. But since I did not, I only can wish that I had at least laughed. There are moments, in ministry and motherhood and simple day-in and day-out life, that do not go as we planned. We are not called to be God. We are called to be humans: living, flawed, and messy humans whom God loves utterly and completely. In those times when things seem like they are falling apart, perhaps we ought to take a step back, chuckle to ourselves, and learn how to offer ourselves and our families the same grace that we are called to extend to our churches and our world.

It won't make our lives perfect. It won't prevent our children from doing ridiculous things at inopportune times. There will be moments of chaos. But grace and laughter and the love of God can help us turn those moments of chaos into something beautiful, real, and blessed. They can take the chaos and shape it and mold it and turn it into something wonderful. And we can receive all of it—the messes and the beauty—for what it truly is: life.

Rev. Kristin Adkins Whitesides was raised as a pastor's kid in Martinsville, Virginia. In 2005, after graduating from the University of Richmond and Duke Divinity School, she was ordained at her home church, Starling Avenue Baptist. Kristin has served as Associate Pastor at First Baptist Church in Winchester, Virginia, since 2005. She and her husband, Sandy, have two sons: Isaac, born in 2007, and Samuel, born in 2011. They lead a chaotic yet happy life together.

.

Other available titles from  SMYTH&HELWYS

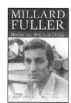

Beyond the American Dream
Millard Fuller

In 1968, Millard finished the story of his journey from pauper to millionaire to home builder. His wife, Linda, occasionally would ask him about getting it published, but Millard would reply, "Not now. I'm too busy." This is that story.   *978-1-57312-563-5 272 pages/pb* **$20.00**

Blissful Affliction
The Ministry and Misery of Writing
Judson Edwards

Edwards draws from more than forty years of writing experience to explore why we use the written word to change lives and how to improve the writing craft.   *978-1-57312-594-9 144 pages/pb* **$15.00**

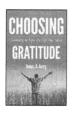

Choosing Gratitude
Learning to Love the Life You Have
James A. Autry

Autry reminds us that gratitude is a choice, a spiritual—not social—process. He suggests that if we cultivate gratitude as a way of being, we may not change the world and its ills, but we can change our response to the world. If we fill our lives with moments of gratitude, we will indeed love the life we have.   *978-1-57312-614-4 144 pages/pb* **$15.00**

Contextualizing the Gospel
A Homiletic Commentary on 1 Corinthians
Brian L. Harbour

Harbour examines every part of Paul's letter, providing a rich resource for those who want to struggle with the difficult texts as well as the simple texts, who want to know how God's word—all of it—intersects with their lives today.   *978-1-57312-589-5 240 pages/pb* **$19.00**

Dance Lessons
Moving to the Beat of God's Heart
Jeanie Miley

Miley shares her joys and struggles a she learns to "dance" with the Spirit of the Living God.   *978-1-57312-622-9 240 pages/pb* **$19.00**

Daniel (Smyth & Helwys Annual Bible Study series)
Keeping Faith When the Heat Is On

Bill Ireland

Daniel is a book about resistance. It was written to people under pressure. In the book, we will see the efforts oppressive regimes take to undermine the faith and identity of God's people. In it, we will also see the strategies God's people employed in resisting the imposition of a foreign culture, and we will see what sustained their efforts. In that vein, the book of Daniel is powerfully relevant. *Teaching Guide 978-1-57312-647-2 144 pages/pb* **$14.00**

Study Guide 978-1-57312-646-5 80 pages/pb **$6.00**

Divorce Ministry
A Guidebook

Charles Qualls

This book shares with the reader the value of establishing a divorce recovery ministry while also offering practical insights on establishing your own unique church-affiliated program. Whether you are working individually with one divorced person or leading a large group, *Divorce Ministry: A Guidebook* provides helpful resources to guide you through the emotional and relational issues divorced people often encounter.

978-1-57312-588-8 156 pages/pb **$16.00**

The Enoch Factor
The Sacred Art of Knowing God

Steve McSwain

The Enoch Factor is a persuasive argument for a more enlightened religious dialogue in America, one that affirms the goals of all religions—guiding followers in self-awareness, finding serenity and happiness, and discovering what the author describes as "the sacred art of knowing God." *978-1-57312-556-7 256 pages/pb* **$21.00**

Healing Our Hurts
Coping with Difficult Emotions

Daniel Bagby

In *Healing Our Hurts*, Daniel Bagby identifies and explains all the dynamics at play in these complex emotions. Offering practical biblical insights to these feelings, he interprets faith-based responses to separate overly religious piety from true, natural human emotion. This book helps us learn how to deal with life's difficult emotions in a redemptive and responsible way. *978-1-57312-613-7 144 pages/pb* **$15.00**

Hope for the Thinking Christian
Seeking a Path of Faith through Everyday Life
Stephen Reese

Readers who want to confront their faith more directly, to think it through and be open to God in an individual, authentic, spiritual encounter will find a resonant voice in Stephen Reese.

978-1-57312-553-6 160 pages/pb **$16.00**

A Hungry Soul Desperate to Taste God's Grace
Honest Prayers for Life
Charles Qualls

Part of how we *see* God is determined by how we *listen* to God. There is so much noise and movement in the world that competes with images of God. This noise would drown out God's beckoning voice and distract us. We may not sense what spiritual directors refer to as the *thin place*—God come near. Charles Qualls's newest book offers readers prayers for that journey toward the meaning and mystery of God. *978-1-57312-648-9 152 pages/pb* **$14.00**

James (Smyth & Helwys Annual Bible Study series)
Being Right in a Wrong World
Michael D. McCullar

Unlike Paul, who wrote primarily to congregations defined by Gentile believers, James wrote to a dispersed and persecuted fellowship of Hebrew Christians who would soon endure even more difficulty in the coming years. *Teaching Guide 1-57312-604-5 160 pages/ pb* **$14.00**
Study Guide 1-57312-605-2 96 pages/pb **$6.00**

James M. Dunn and Soul Freedom
Aaron Douglas Weaver

James Milton Dunn, over the last fifty years, has been the most aggressive Baptist proponent for religious liberty in the United States. Soul freedom—voluntary, uncoerced faith and an unfettered individual conscience before God—is the basis of his understanding of church-state separation and the historic Baptist basis of religious liberty.

978-1-57312-590-1 224 pages/pb **$18.00**

The Jesus Tribe
Following Christ in the Land of the Empire
Ronnie McBrayer

The Jesus Tribe fleshes out the implications, possibilities, contradictions, and complexities of what it means to live within the Jesus Tribe and in the shadow of the American Empire.

978-1-57312-592-5 208 pages/pb **$17.00**

Joint Venture

Jeanie Miley

Joint Venture is a memoir of the author's journey to find and express her inner, authentic self, not as an egotistical venture, but as a sacred responsibility and partnership with God. Miley's quest for Christian wholeness is a rich resource for other seekers.

978-1-57312-581-9 224 pages/pb **$17.00**

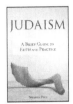

Judaism
A Brief Guide to Faith and Practice

Sharon Pace

Sharon Pace's newest book is a sensitive and comprehensive intro-duction to Judaism. What is it like to be born into the Jewish community? How does belief in the One God and a universal morality shape the way in which Jews see the world? How does one find meaning in life and the courage to endure suffering? How does one mark joy and forge com-munity ties?

978-1-57312-644-1 144 pages/pb **$16.00**

Lessons from the Cloth 2
501 More One Minute Motivators for Leaders

Bo Prosser and Charles Qualls

As the force that drives organizations to accomplishment, leader-ship is at a crucial point in churches, corporations, families, and almost every arena of life. Without leadership there is chaos. *With* leadership there is sometimes chaos! In this follow-up to their first volume, Bo Prosser and Charles Qualls will inspire you to keep growing in your leadership career.

978-1-57312-665-6 152 pages/pb **$11.00**

Let Me More of Their Beauty See
Reading Familiar Verses in Context

Diane G. Chen

Let Me More of Their Beauty See offers eight examples of how atten-tion to the historical and literary settings can safeguard against taking a text out of context, bring out its transforming power in greater dimension, and help us apply Scripture appropriately in our daily lives.

978-1-57312-564-2 160 pages/pb **$17.00**

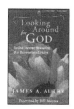

Looking Around for God
The Strangely Reverent Observations of an Unconventional Christian
James A. Autry

Looking Around for God, Autry's tenth book, is in many ways his most personal. In it he considers his unique life of faith and belief in God. Autry is a former Fortune 500 executive, author, poet, and consultant whose work has had a significant influence on leadership thinking.

978-157312-484-3 144 pages/pb **$16.00**

Maggie Lee for Good
Jinny and John Hinson

Maggie Lee for Good captures the essence of a young girl's boundless faith and spirit. Her parents' moving story of the accident that took her life will inspire readers who are facing loss, looking for evidence of God's sustaining grace, or searching for ways to make a meaningful difference in the lives of others.

978-1-57312-630-4 144 pages/pb **$15.00**

Making the Timeless Word Timely
A Primer for Preachers
Michael B. Brown

Michael Brown writes, "There is a simple formula for sermon preparation that creates messages that apply and engage whether your parish is rural or urban, young or old, rich or poor, five thousand members or fifty." The other part of the task, of course, involves being creative and insightful enough to know how to take the general formula for sermon preparation and make it particular in its impact on a specific congregation. Brown guides the reader through the formula and the skills to employ it with excellence and integrity.

978-1-57312-578-9 160 pages/pb **$16.00**

The Ministry Life
101 Tips for New Ministers
John Killinger

Sharing years of wisdom from more than fifty years in ministry and teaching, *The Ministry Life: 101 Tips for New Ministers* by John Killinger is filled with practical advice and wisdom for a minister's day-to-day tasks as well as advice on intellectual and spiritual habits to keep ministers of any age healthy and fulfilled.

978-1-57312-662-5 244 pages/pb **$19.00**

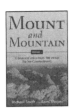

Mount and Mountain
Vol. 1: A Reverend and a Rabbi Talk About the Ten Commandments

Rami Shapiro and Michael Smith

Mount and Mountain represents the first half of an interfaith dialogue—a dialogue that neither preaches nor placates but challenges its participants to work both singly and together in the task of reinterpreting sacred texts. Mike and Rami discuss the nature of divinity, the power of faith, the beauty of myth and story, the necessity of doubt, the achievements, failings, and future of religion, and, above all, the struggle to live ethically and in harmony with the way of God.   978-1-57312-612-0 144 pages/pb **$15.00**

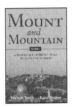

Mount and Mountain
Vol. 2: A Reverend and a Rabbi Talk About the Sermon on the Mount

Rami Shapiro and Michael Smith

This book, focused on the Sermon on the Mount, represents the second half of Mike and Rami's dialogue. In it, Mike and Rami explore the text of Jesus' sermon cooperatively, contributing perspectives drawn from their lives and religious traditions and seeking moments of illumination.   978-1-57312-654-0 254 pages/pb **$19.00**

Overcoming Adolescence
Growing Beyond Childhood into Maturity

Marion D. Aldridge

In *Overcoming Adolescence*, Marion Aldridge poses questions for adults of all ages to consider. His challenge to readers is one he has personally worked to confront: to grow up *all the way*—mentally, physically, academically, socially, emotionally, and spiritually. The key involves not only knowing how to work through the process but also how to recognize what may be contributing to our perpetual adolescence.

978-1-57312-577-2 156 pages/pb **$17.00**

Psychic Pancakes & Communion Pizza
More Musings and Mutterings of a Church Misfit

Bert Montgomery

Psychic Pancakes & Communion Pizza is Bert Montgomery's highly anticipated follow-up to *Elvis, Willie, Jesus & Me* and contains further reflections on music, film, culture, life, and finding Jesus in the midst of it all.   978-1-57312-578-9 160 pages/pb **$16.00**

To order call **1-800-747-3016** or visit **www.helwys.com**

Reading Ezekiel (Reading the Old Testament series)
A Literary and Theological Commentary
Marvin A Sweeney

The book of Ezekiel points to the return of YHWH to the holy temple at the center of a reconstituted Israel and creation at large. As such, the book of Ezekiel portrays the purging of Jerusalem, the Temple, and the people, to reconstitute them as part of a new creation at the conclusion of the book. With Jerusalem, the Temple, and the people so purged, YHWH stands once again in the holy center of the created world.

978-1-57312-658-8 264 pages/pb **$22.00**

Reading Job (Reading the Old Testament series)
A Literary and Theological Commentary
James L. Crenshaw

At issue in the Book of Job is a question with which most all of us struggle at some point in life, "Why do bad things happen to good people?" James Crenshaw has devoted his life to studying the disturbing matter of theodicy—divine justice—that troubles many people of faith.

978-1-57312-574-1 192 pages/pb **$22.00**

Reading Judges (Reading the Old Testament series)
A Literary and Theological Commentary
Mark E. Biddle

Reading the Old Testament book of Judges presents a number of significant challenges related to social contexts, historical settings, and literary characteristics. Acknowledging and examining these difficulties provides a point of entry into the world of Judges and promises to enrich the reading experience.

978-1-57312-631-1 240 pages/pb **$22.00**

Reading Samuel (Reading the Old Testament series)
A Literary and Theological Commentary
Johanna W. H. van Wijk-Bos

Interpreted masterfully by preeminent Old Testament scholar Johanna W. H. van Wijk-Bos, the story of Samuel touches on a vast array of subjects that make up the rich fabric of human life. The reader gains an inside look at leadership, royal intrigue, military campaigns, occult practices, and the significance of religious objects of veneration.

978-1-57312-607-6 272 pages/pb **$22.00**

The Role of the Minister in a Dying Congregation
Lynwood B. Jenkins

Jenkins provides a courageous and responsible resource on one of the most critical issues in congregational life: how to help a congregation conclude its ministry life cycle with dignity and meaning.

978-1-57312-571-0 96 pages/pb **$14.00**

Sessions with Genesis (Session Bible Studies series)
The Story Begins
Tony W. Cartledge

Immersing us in the book of Genesis, Tony Cartledge examines both its major stories and the smaller cycles of hope and failure, of promise and judgment. Genesis introduces these themes of divine faithfulness and human failure in unmistakable terms, tracing Israel's beginning to the creation of the world and professing a belief that Israel's particular history had universal significance.

978-1-57312-636-6 144 pages/pb **$14.00**

Sessions with Philippians (Session Bible Studies series)
Finding Joy in Community
Bo Prosser

In this brief letter to the Philippians, Paul makes clear the centrality of his faith in Jesus Christ, his love for the Philippian church, and his joy in serving both Christ and their church.

978-1-57312-579-6 112 pages/pb **$13.00**

Sessions with Samuel (Session Bible Studies series)
Stories from the Edge
Tony W. Cartledge

In these stories, Israel faces one crisis after another, a people constantly on the edge. Individuals such as Saul and David find themselves on the edge as well, facing troubles of leadership and personal struggle. Yet, each crisis becomes a gateway for learning that God is always present, that hope remains.

978-1-57312-555-0 112 pages/pb **$13.00**

Silver Linings
My Life Before and After Challenger 7
June Scobee Rodgers

We know the public story of *Challenger 7*'s tragic destruction. That day, June's life took a new direction that ultimately led to the creation of the Challenger Center and to new life and new love. Her story of Christian faith and triumph over adversity will inspire readers of every age.

978-1-57312-570-3 352 pages/hc **$28.00**

Spacious
Exploring Faith and Place
Holly Sprink

Exploring where we are and why that matters to God is an ongoing process. If we are present and attentive, God creatively and continuously widens our view of the world, whether we live in the Amazon or in our own hometown. *978-1-57312-649-6 156 pages/pb* **$16.00**

This Is What a Preacher Looks Like
Sermons by Baptist Women in Ministry
Pamela Durso, ed.

In this collection of sermons by thirty-six Baptist women, their voices are soft and loud, prophetic and pastoral, humorous and sincere. They are African American, Asian, Latina, and Caucasian. They are sisters, wives, mothers, grandmothers, aunts, and friends.

978-1-57312-554-3 144 pages/pb **$18.00**

Transformational Leadership
Leading with Integrity
Charles B. Bugg

"Transformational" leadership involves understanding and growing so that we can help create positive change in the world. This book encourages leaders to be willing to change if *they* want to help transform the world. They are honest about their personal strengths and weaknesses, and are not afraid of doing a fearless moral inventory of themselves.

978-1-57312-558-1 112 pages/pb **$14.00**

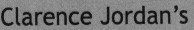